ABOUT FREDERICK BUECHNER

Frederick Buechner brings the reader to his knees, sometimes in laughter, sometimes in an astonishment very close to prayer, and at the best of times in a combination of both.

The New York Times Book Review

With profound intelligence, Buechner's novel does what the finest, most appealing literature does: it displays and illuminates the seemingly unrelated mysteries of human character and ultimate ideas . . . One of our finest writers.

Annie Dillard, *Boston Globe*

If Frederick Buechner subordinated his nature and chose to write on naughts and nothings, he would still exalt his readers. When he is in representative harmony and writes of the accessibility of God to humanity and of humanity's agreement with its potential divinity, we, the readers, are lifted up, buoyed up, and promised wholeness.

Maya Angelou

You don't have to be in the habit of going to church to listen to such a literary minister; you don't have to be a believer to be moved by Mr. Buechner's faith.

John Irving

Frederick Buechner is a beacon. When we can't remember what is true and what it all means, he's the person we turn to.

Anne Lamott

Frederick Buechner has inspired me not only with his writing, but with his generosity of spirit. I'm incredibly thankful.

Rachel Held Evans

He isn't trying to persuade—he's trying to understand what he himself believes and thinks. And that honesty is more persuasive than the most polished argument.

John Ortberg

Frederick Buechner doesn't just show us how to write; he shows us how to live.

Philip Yancey

Frederick Buechner is not just a wordsmith but an image-smith—he's the bridge between Gutenberg and Google.

Len Sweet

To each new generation, his work is a revelation.

The Lutheran

Frederick Buechner gives new life to Christian truth.

Katelyn Beaty

He raises the bar not only for Christian writers, but for all of literature.

Mako Fujimura

A CRAZY, HOLY GRACE

Also by Frederick Buechner

A CRAZY, HOLY GRACE

The Healing Power of Pain and Memory

FREDERICK BUECHNER

ZONDERVAN

A Crazy, Holy Grace
Copyright © 2017 by Frederick Buechner Literary Assets, LLC

Requests for information should be addressed to:
Zondervan, *3900 Sparks Dr. SE, Grand Rapids, Michigan 49546*

ISBN 978-0-310-35162-7 (audio)

ISBN 978-0-310-35054-5 (ebook)

Library of Congress Cataloging-in-Publication Data
Names: Buechner, Frederick, 1926- author.
Title: A crazy, holy grace : the healing power of pain and memory / Frederick
    Buechner.
Description: Grand Rapids, Michigan : Zondervan, [2017] | Includes bibliographical
    references.
Identifiers: LCCN 2017024954 | ISBN 9780310349761 (softcover)
Subjects: LCSH: Pain—Religious aspects—Christianity. | Suffering—Religious
    aspects—Christianity.
Classification: LCC BV4909 .B83 2017 | DDC 248.8/6—dc23 LC record available
    at https://lccn.loc.gov/2017024954

Art direction: Curt Diepenhorst
Interior design: Denise Froehlich
Zondervan Editorial: John Sloan, Robert Hudson, Gwyneth Findlay

First printing August 2017 / Printed in the United States of America

CONTENTS

FOREWORD

It seems that pain and death are on the rise, lurking in the shadows, waiting to pounce, ready or not. Our lives are filled with freak accidents, cancer, and the steady decay of time. Stories of destruction and pain come at us from everywhere—our news, TV shows, movies, and social media sites—because fear and death seem to sell even more than sex. Under such a barrage of tragedy, hope can seem a flimsy comfort or, at best, a hole in the ground you can stick your head into, like an ostrich. Is it real? Is God really there? Or are we just fooling ourselves in order to cope?

My mentor and friend Dale Brown was someone whose loss I felt deeply, suddenly. There is still a Dale Brown-shaped hole in the world; I can't often think of him without tears springing to my eyes. I didn't see him all that much, but somehow it seemed as if the world would be all right in the end with him around. I met Dale at Calvin College in Grand Rapids, Michigan, when I took his class in modern literature. He introduced me to Frederick Buechner and showed me how Buechner's early writings straddle the shift between modern and postmodern eras in Western literature. As our culture shifts again from postmodernism into something post-Christian, Buechner's voice has never been more relevant. Though he wrote almost everything in the twentieth century, he is a sort of twenty-first-century C. S. Lewis, speaking about truth and hope and faith in a way that resonates with the faithful and the faith-suspicious alike. And he tells the truth in stories we want to read more than once.

The dread pirate Roberts in *The Princess Bride* famously points out to Princess Buttercup, "Life *is* pain, highness. Anyone who says differently is selling something." The statement is true, and useful for adjusting our expectations, but it leaves us emptyhanded when life takes a turn and the ones we love, or we ourselves, suffer and die. What Buechner does, and why I keep coming back to him year after year, is to say we will all of us lose everything and everyone we love. We don't know, really *know*, what comes next. True hope is hard won, and the struggle to hang on to it is more than we can often bear. But Buechner says if we will simply quiet ourselves and really listen into the stillness and silence, we will hear God speaking to us. In the quiet, we can use our memories and imaginations to remember our stories and the lives of our lost loved ones. And then we can catch glimpses of him who was there all along.

As Buechner's fictional character Godric says, "What's lost is nothing to what's found, and all the death that ever was, set next to life, would scarcely fill a cup." It was Dale Brown's favorite Buechner quote. It sticks with me still: "All the death that ever was, set next to life, would scarcely fill a cup. . . . All's lost. All's found."

And that's what this new collection of Buechner's writings, including a lecture he gave that has never before appeared in print, aims to help us realize—that when we enter the gates of pain and use the healing power of memory, we will hear God speaking, and we can take comfort and rest our weary souls in his crazy, holy grace.

CALEB J. SEELING, EDITOR
GOLDEN, COLORADO

A CRAZY, HOLY GRACE

PART 1

PAIN AND THE CRAZY, HOLY GRACE OF GOD

CHAPTER 1

THE GATES
OF PAIN

When I woke up this morning, before I'd gotten out of bed, I was looking around to see what was going on in my room. Not much was going on, I'm happy to say. But there was a cricket on the glazed stone floor. He didn't belong in the room. Crickets don't belong in rooms. I looked at him and decided to give him a helping hand, so I picked him up as gently as I could so as not to either alarm him or hurt him, and I carried him out into the sunshine. And he hopped away to do whatever crickets do, where they belong. And I thought to myself, that's what it's all about: to be lifted up carefully and in a way not to frighten us, to be taken out of the confinement of the room where we're locked up away from where we belong, and to be carried out into the fresh air. And that's, in a way I guess, what this book is about, how to get out of that room or what to do when you're in that room.

I don't speak often about my father's drinking. He wasn't a raging drunk. He didn't go around smashing furniture and punching people in the nose. Rather, I think drinking was one of the ways he survived his life. Especially when he went out to parties, he would drink too much. When he would come back, as much as I can remember him, which is dimly, he was another person. He was sort of scary and sad.

One night, he had been drinking, and he decided he wanted to go away somewhere in the car. My mother said something like, "You can't do that. You'll kill yourself or smash up the car," and she somehow got hold of the keys. She gave them to me and said, "Whatever else you do, don't give them to your father." I was in bed, and I remember gripping the keys in my hand. There were two twin beds—I was in one with the covers over my head, scared. My father came into the room, sat on the other bed, and pled for me to give him the keys. I didn't know what to do or what to say or what to be or what to think or what to do. I just remember, sort of dimly, his voice saying, "Please give me the keys." And I, of course, said nothing at all. The keys were clenched in my fist under the pillow and the covers were over my head. Eventually I think he went to sleep, and that was the end of that. But, of course, it left a tremendous mark; I can remember it to this very day. That is the kind of shadow side of my childhood.

I told this story to a group in Texas once, and afterward the retreat leader came up to me and said, "You've had a good deal of pain in your life," which, of course, he could've said to any one of us. And he said, "You've been a good steward of it. You've been a good steward of your pain." That caught me absolutely off balance. I've never heard that before. *Steward* has always been a boring, churchy word to me, you know? Stewardship Sunday or something like that. It's about taking care of your money, probably. But to be a steward of your pain, what a marvelous idea. I've thought a great deal about it ever since—what it means to be a steward of your pain, the various ways in which we deal with the sad and puzzling things that happen to us over the course of our lives.

■ ■ ■

Maybe the first thing to say is that pain, of course, is universal. All the great visionaries, the great holy ones, I think have
known that. I think of Siddhartha Gautama, the Buddha, who
when he came out from under the Bodhi Tree, having had his
enlightenment, uttered the four noble truths of Buddhism, of
which the first is "All life is suffering, all life is pain." And of the
four noble truths, certainly none is truer than that.

I wish I could talk more about what he said about pain, but
I'm not going to get into that. Simply put, suffering is universal.
Pain is what it's all about. Life is terminal. We all end up in
death or losing everything we have and are and love. And I think
that when Jesus looked out at the world of young people and
old people, lucky people, unlucky people, black people, white
people, poor people, rich people, and said, "Come unto me, all
ye that labour and are heavy laden, and I will give you rest," he
was saying some of the same thing. No matter who you are, how
lucky or unlucky, or rich or poor, or this or that, part of what
it means to be a human being in this world is to labor and be
heavy laden, to be in need of whatever he means by rest.

The universality of pain. The fraternity, the sorority of pain.
We all know what it's about. We're all in it. And there are all
sorts of different ways of dealing with it. Who knows how many
there are, and when you cut them up fine and say there's this
one and that one and the other one, that they are really as sepa-
rate as that? We all have different ways of dealing with our pain,
depending on what day it happens to be and how we happen to
be feeling. But it seems to me that it is worth mentioning what
I think of as sort of the principal ways of dealing with the sad
things that happen, the bad, wretched things that happen.

One of them, the one that was certainly the one that my family tended to choose, and that I think most dysfunctional families tend to choose, is to deal with your pain by simply forgetting it. Shutting it away. This is what my mother did. She had not only the suicide of my father but two other unsuccessful marriages. I think it's why she shut so many out. I always suspected her deafness was related to not wanting to hear the word of judgment that she felt the world was passing upon her for having had these bad marriages. I think part of the reason she closed her eyes when she talked to people was she didn't want to see or, ostrich-like, to be seen somehow. She closed herself off. She dealt with her pain simply by dismissing it. Except from time to time, once in a great while, she'd talk about it. And that is a method of survival. Of course, all these ways of dealing with your pain are methods of surviving your pain, and this is not the worst. It is a way of surviving, and my mother miraculously did survive her pain. She lived to a great age, and in many ways she remained a valuable person. Fun to be with, full of her own kind of life, a wonderful sense of the sort of ridiculousness of being old and lame. That wonderful remark I quoted somewhere, when she was lying in bed in Vermont and she said, "Who just passed by the window?" And I said, "It's the gardener." And she said, "Well, tell him to come have a look at the last rose of summer." Wonderful to be able to say that when you are the last rose of summer. So she survived. And she survived as a human being, despite all the reasons she might have had for becoming something less than human.

But I think that the price that one pays by dealing with your pain by forgetting it, by stuffing it aside, by not looking at it, is that some part of you doesn't grow. I think the part of her that didn't grow was what might have been the compassionate part of her, the part of her that by sort of looking at her own pain would have opened her up to the sense that other people were in pain, and then she might have been able to reach out into other people's lives. She never did. She had friends, but I can't imagine her ever having had a friend for whom she would've sacrificed herself. That whole part of her didn't grow. The most human part of her that might have been never really came to be because of all the things she sort of stuffed aside, the things that might have opened her.

So that's one way. Bad things happen. Painful things happen, and you survive them by simply getting on as if they hadn't happened at all.

Another way, I think, is to be somehow trapped by your pain. Being stopped in your tracks. Never, in a sense, being able to escape your pain. Never being able to move on out of it into whatever lies beyond. I think a classic example of that would be the character Miss Havisham in Charles Dickens's *Great Expectations*. Miss Havisham was at an early age all set to be married. She had on her bridal finery, and the great wedding cake was there in the parlor. Then her boyfriend jilted her, and that was the end of her life. From that day on, she lived in that room, wearing her tattered, moldering wedding clothes, with the cake still there, a sort of ruined pile on the table with cobwebs and mice. And I think I've known people like that, who have been somehow trapped in their pain. It becomes their confinement. It becomes like the room to the cricket—it can't get out of it. You keep living it over and over and over again, almost relishing the bitterness of it. So you deal with your pain by allowing it to overwhelm you, by allowing it to stop you in your tracks. And I suppose it's also a way of surviving your pain, because as in the case of Miss Havisham, you take a kind of grim, awful pleasure in your ruin.

19

Another Dickens character comes to mind (he was such a great caricaturist) from *David Copperfield*. Mrs. Gummidge, who was related to the Peggottys and lived in that overturned dory on the beach. And the line she speaks is in sort of a wispy voice, "I'm a lone lorn creetur." She's a widow, and she has a black silk handkerchief into which she weeps continually. It's another way of dealing with pain, as if her pain is the biggest thing that's ever happened to her, her justification for existing. The fact that she's a "lone lorn creetur"—a lone, lost creature— becomes almost a kind of achievement. It's what she is known by. It's what she justifies her life by. It's what she presents. You feel it's almost an excuse for her to never become anything else. She's had this grief, whatever it is, and that's what her life's been all about, and that's all that it needs to be about.

The other day I was in another one of these speaking jamborees, and the daughter of an old friend of mine came to see me. She told me a horror story about her marriage—her husband had been diagnosed with premature dementia. He'd lost all sense of judgment. He would disappear for days because he wanted to get a book out of the library and the city was six hundred miles away. He didn't bother to tell her where he was. He'd lost all their money, and they were being sued by their various creditors to the point that she finally divorced her husband, though she still lives with him, because otherwise what little money she had would be liable to be taken. It's just a hopeless story. I could see nothing in it that suggested there was any way out of it. But as she told it, she kept laughing this awful, chill, unearthly, inhuman laugh, as if her way of surviving her pain was to make a kind of a joke out of it: "Guess what's happened to me, and guess what all has come about?" It made it almost impossible to talk to her seriously about these *good steward of pain*

terrible things because, in a way, she was holding them off. ③
The method by which she held them off was this kind of grim
gallows laughter. She made a joke out of it. She hid her pain
behind the joke. The joke was there, but the pain that the joke
was about had somehow been covered up. She'd allowed it, or
encouraged it, to creep off into the wings.

Then lastly, the one that I thought of the other day was com-
petitive pain: "You think you've had it bad? Let me tell you what's
happened to me!" Pain becomes a kind of accomplishment.
What have I done with my life? I've suffered like hell, and if you
think *you've* suffered, let me tell you how *I've* suffered."

■ ■ ■

I'm sure there are a hundred and six other ways we have of
coping with pain. I think at one time or another each one of
us has probably coped with it in all of those ways. One day,
one way; another day, another way. Certainly years ago, and I
suppose to a degree still, I dealt with the sad parts of my life by
forgetting them. I didn't know I was forgetting them. I didn't
say to myself, "I'm going to forget them," but the mechanism of
forgetting had been so strongly switched on in my childhood
that it became a sort of automatic response. ④

Another way of dealing with your pain is to be a good
steward of it.

Let me remind you of one of the most familiar of all of Jesus's
parables, the Parable of the Talents, which goes as follows:

> "For it will be as when a man going on a journey called his
> servants and entrusted to them his property; to one he gave
> five talents, to another two, to another one, to each accord-
> ing to his ability. Then he went away. He who had received

21

the five talents went at once and traded with them; and he made five talents more. So also, he who had the two talents made two talents more. But he who had received the one talent went and dug in the ground and hid his master's money. Now after a long time the master of those servants came and settled accounts with them. And he who had received the five talents came forward, bringing five talents more, saying, 'Master, you delivered to me five talents; here I have made five talents more.' His master said to him, 'Well done, good and faithful servant; you have been faithful over a little, I will set you over much; enter into the joy of your master.' And he also who had the two talents came forward, saying, 'Master, you delivered to me two talents; here I have made two talents more.' His master said to him, 'Well done, good and faithful servant; you have been faithful over a little, I will set you over much; enter into the joy of your master.' He also who had received the one talent came forward, saying, 'Master, I knew you to be a hard man, reaping where you did not sow, and gathering where you did not winnow; so I was afraid, and I went and hid your talent in the ground. Here you have what is yours.' But his master answered him, 'You wicked and slothful servant! You knew that I reap where I have not sowed, and gather where I have not winnowed? Then you ought to have invested my money with the bankers, and at my coming I should have received what was my own with interest. So take the talent from him, and give it to him who has the ten talents. For to every one who has will more be given, and he will have abundance; but from him who has not, even what he has will be taken away. And cast the worthless servant into the outer darkness; there men will weep and gnash their teeth.'" (Matthew 25:14–30)

These extraordinary parables of Jesus, who could ever guess that that's the way the story was going to end? If you and I had written it in our boring way, we would've rewarded the man, wouldn't we? At least I think I would've. He seems like the sensible one that didn't take risks with his talent. But that's not the way the story goes. It's a dark and frightening and fascinating story.

I don't know how you read it, but I take the talents—one gets five, one gets two, one gets one—as whatever it is that life deals us. It's the hand we're dealt at birth. Some are born white, some are born black. Some are born in one country, some in another country. Some are born into families that don't know what in hell is going on and are dysfunctional and do terrible things; some are born into families where there seems to be a kind of peace. So the world gives us a little hand of cards, and then we're left to play with them. I think that's what the parable is about.

The way in which these three people handle what they've been given is important. The one to start with, I think, because it's the most striking part of the parable, the most frightening part, is the poor soul who took his one talent and buried it in the ground and met such a terrible fate. He explains why he buried it, saying to the master, "I was afraid." _I was afraid_. And I think of the master as God, or you would think about the master as life itself who dealt the hand. "I knew you to be a hard man, and I was afraid. What if I lost the talent?"

And, of course, he was right. God is a hard God in many ways, who says, "Be perfect, even as your father in heaven is perfect." That's a hard rule: to be perfect, even as your father in heaven is perfect. I think of the first epistle of John, that devastating law that is set down, "He who does not love, remains in death." That's a hard saying. In other words, not to love is in a sense to die. He was right, the man with the one talent, to be afraid. There is much in life—there is much in the nature of God as we understand him—of which to be afraid. He asks a great deal of us.

So in fear, being afraid—afraid of his life, afraid of living, afraid of making use of his talents, afraid to do the wrong thing, afraid of whatever he's afraid of—he takes it and he buries it. He buries what he'd been given. He buries his experience. And the master is angry.

The one-talent man says another thing that seems to be so revealing: "You're a hard man, reaping where you did not sow and gathering where you did not winnow." As I understand that, God does not sow the field of our life. He does not make these things happen. He did not cause Chester's car to smash into Paula's car, killing her young husband and her daughter. God doesn't deal with the world that way; he doesn't move us around like chess pieces. He does not sow, but he expects that out of whatever the world in its madness does to us, we will somehow reap a harvest. He does not sow these things that happen, but he expects us to deal with these things in creative and redemptive and life-opening sorts of ways. But again, the one-talent man was right, God does reap where he did not sow. He gathers where he did not winnow. He does not sow the pain, he does not make the pain happen, but he looks to us to harvest treasure from the pain. Like the girl in the fairytale, he looks for us to spin gold out of the straw of what happens to us.

Then the master speaks his word of darkness. He looks at the one-talent man and calls him a wicked and slothful servant. Because, of all the seven deadly sins, sloth is not only the one that this one-talent man is guilty of, but it may be the worst of the sins. Sloth. You think of all the others as much worse than that—lust, anger, pride, and so on—but sloth is what this man is condemned for. Sloth is getting through life on automatic pilot. Not really being alive. Not really making use of what happens to you. Burying what you might have made something out of. Playing it safe with your life. To bury your life, to bury your pain, to bury your joy. To bury whatever it is that the world gives you, and then live as carefully as you can without really living at all. And I think that when the master speaks of being cast into darkness, whether it was wailing and gnashing of teeth, it's not so much that he's saying, "I'm going to punish you by casting you into the darkness where you will wail and gnash your teeth," but, "To live a buried life is to say you have not really lived your life at all." To live closed up in yourself, as that cricket was closed up in the room, is itself wailing and gnashing of teeth. The buried life is a lonely life, a dark life, a Miss Havisham life. And I think, in some measure, we all know what that means because there's part of all of our lives that we choose not to live out of one kind of timidity or the other.

And then the ultimate word of judgment that the master speaks is, "From him who has not, even what he has will be taken away." This from, you must remember, the Prince of Peace, the Good Shepherd. From him who has not, even what he has will be taken. That seems the ultimate injustice, to take away the one talent from a man who has only one talent and give it to the other ones. I take that to mean, again, not a punishment so much as the inevitable consequence of burying your life. If you bury your life—if you don't face, among other things, your pain—your life shrinks. It is in a way diminished. It is in a way taken away.

Like my mother, by burying so much of the sadness of her life, her life was diminished. She never grew in the way she might have. She never became the human being she richly had it in her to become. She never became the compassionate, outward-reaching person who had real friends. Her life shrunk. Talk about life as parable. She took her name out of the telephone book, not hearing, not seeing, rarely leaving her apartment. First her apartment, then her bedroom, then her chair in her bedroom, and finally her bed—it was just this sort of gradual shrinking. *From him who has not, even what he has will be taken away.* That's not punishing the one-talent man so much as to say to him, "That's what happens when you do not live your life, when you do not harvest your pain. You have less life every day."

And then, of course, there are the other servants who put their money out to earn interest, whom the master calls good and faithful servants. Faithful, as if their goodness is their faithfulness. They somehow—despite the fact that the master was a hard master, despite the fact that God makes impossible demands of us or terrible demands of us: to be perfect, to be loving, to be open—have faith in him that somehow all will be well; that it's worth taking the risk, even if you live your life and it doesn't turn out the way you want. There is forgiveness. There is compassion. There is mercy in God. And therefore, you dare take your chances and do what you can do with the hand that life, or God, has dealt you.

So what they did, those other two servants, as Jesus's story described it, they went and traded with their talents. And I think the word *trade* is a significant word. They took what had been given them and they traded with it. They were not life-buriers like that first fellow. They were life-traders. They traded life for life. What does it mean to trade? I think it means to

26

give of what you have in return for what you need. You give of yourself, and in return you receive something from other selves to whom you give.

■ ■ ■

I can think of no better example than in my own recent life. Once during the illness of my oldest daughter, who had ano-rexia almost to the point of death, a friend of mine—a very recent friend, I didn't know him awfully well—knew about this trouble in my life. He was a minister in Charlotte, North Carolina, where I'd been on some sort of speaking thing. And one day in Vermont, the phone rang. I picked it up and here was my friend on the other end. And I said, "Oh my golly, Lou, how nice to hear from you. How are things in Charlotte?" He said, "Well, I'm not in Charlotte. I'm in Manchester." Manchester, Vermont, is perhaps fifteen minutes away from where I live. And I said, "What do you mean you're in Manchester?" And he said, "Yeah, I knew it was a bad time for you; I just thought it might be nice to have somebody, an extra friend, around." And I just thought, *My God, I might not even have been here.* Of course, if he'd called me ahead of time and said, "I think I'll come up to see you," I would've said, "Don't even dream of such a preposterous thing." I wouldn't have allowed it. He knew that. So instead, he came eight hundred miles in an air-plane and found himself a room at a hotel, taking the chance that I would be there, which I was. And I was moved to the very soles of my feet by that experience. And so was he, of course. So was he.

It was a trading of lives, where he gave me of himself and received from me of myself. What a sense of peace we had. We didn't talk about holy matters. We didn't talk about religious things. We didn't talk about anything much at all. We smoked on our pipes in the woods and took walks. He was there a couple of days, but it was a blessed event, a holy event, because he had been willing to trade with his life. A good and faithful servant trading with his talents.

It's natural to trade with joy, you know. "I couldn't contain my joy." It's a wonderful expression. I couldn't contain it; I had to say something about it. You go to a football game and somebody makes a marvelous run or something, and you say, "My God, did you see that?" And you slap the fellow on the back beside you. "Look at that wonderful thing!" You have to share joy. It's almost part of what joy is, the desire to share it.

But it's not so natural to share the pain, to trade with the pain. And yet, I think that is what the parable is saying—to trade with pain. To not do any of those things that I listed in the beginning as ways of surviving it, but rather open it.

I think, of course, of the twelve-step programs, which is what they're all about. They are places where people come together saying, "We cannot cope with our own sadness, our own bad memories, without each other and without our higher power, whatever that higher power happens to be." And people sit around in a room—and the magic of those programs to me is nobody advises anybody, nobody lectures anybody, there's no little homily—where everybody simply talks out of his or her own experience of somehow having not just survived their sad times, but having somewhat grown through them. And you realize to what degree that story is your story. Miracles happen because of the willingness to open the door into your pain. *Open your ears and your eyes* to the elusive, invisible, silent presence of healing, of the power of God to heal, which moves as quietly, as undramatically, as the wind moves.

28

■ ■ ■

You know, there are times when you wish that Jesus had a hand of flesh to take hold of. But there isn't one—Jesus has no flesh hands anymore, except insofar as he has your and my hands. And yet there is the sense, from time to time, of his presence. When my daughter was dying, in effect, in this hospital on the west coast, I had never lived through a time when, in any obvious way, God seemed more distant. This girl reduced to a concentration camp victim, her arms and legs such sticks, her lovely young face such a death head that when we came upon her in the hospital that first night after we arrived, I literally would not have known it was my daughter. It was a horrifying, terrifying time. Which might well have given rise to the sense of, "If there is a God, what in hell is going on? How does this kind of thing get to happen?" But instead, by grace, I had this overpowering kind of comfort. God was silent. He said nothing I could hear; he did nothing I could see. But I had this tremendous sense that he was doing all he could do without blowing the whole show sky-high. The way Shakespeare does all he can do with *Hamlet* without somehow entering *Hamlet* and therefore destroying the whole play-ness of the play. I sensed so much the passionate restraint and hush of God. As I dream him, he wants so much to be able to step in and make things right, but how can God do that without destroying what life is all about? If God started stepping in and setting things right, what happens to us? We cease to be human beings. We cease to be free. We cease to be people who can do one thing or another thing with the talents we're given. We become chess pieces on a chessboard. But I sensed the passionate restraint in the silence of God, which was both silent and yet eloquent.

And as I say, he spoke no word that I could hear; he did nothing that I could see. But two things happened during that time when we were living in a hotel in Seattle and going every day to see this sick daughter. One thing was, out of nowhere came two men, Bill Welch and Paul Beaman, may their names be praised. Both were ministers, it turned out, who, by some grapevine, had heard of what was going on and just appeared out of nowhere. Like dreams. They offered no suffocating good advice or platitudinous explanations of why bad things happen to reasonably good people. They just were there. They took us out to lunch and told us about the cathedral in Seattle, where there was a wonderful vespers service where my wife and I went. They were life-givers, life-savers, sent by God, I suspect. I don't mean sent in the sense that he moved them there, but something in the mysterious air of the world wafted them there, because that air, like the rest of the world, proceeds from the mouth of God.

And the other thing that happened was when I played that old sort of fortune-telling trick with the Bible. I was so desperate, I said, "Why not?" So I just let it fall open. And of course, more often than not it falls to Psalms because that's the middle of the Bible where Bibles are apt to fall open. But it fell open to a psalm I had never read before; at least, if I had read it I had not read it, really. It was Psalm 131, which says,

> O Lord, my heart is not lifted up,
>   my eyes are not raised too high;
> I do not occupy myself with things
>   too great and too marvelous for me.
> But I have calmed and quieted my soul,
>   like a child quieted at its mother's breast;
>   like a child that is quieted is my soul.

border walker   depth diver

O Israel, hope in the Lord
from this time forth and for evermore.

But of all Psalms, it was the psalm I needed. My eyes were not lifted up, my heart was not high. I was not occupying myself with anything except how I was going to survive the sight of my child. And yet, with God here presented not as a he but as a she, there was some sense in which I was quieted like a child at its mother's breast. And that psalm was my talisman, my magic talisman, helping to see me through that bad time.

I'm talking now about what it means to trade with your pain, as the good and faithful servants traded with their talents. The help I got from those two people, and the help I got from God, was the help I was able to get because I knew so desperately I needed help. That was my part of the transaction. "Help me!" "All right," they said, "here is some help."

It's hard to share not just the shallows of your life, which is what we're all so good at doing, but to speak out of the depths of your life—the depths are scary. To go down into the depths of your past, to go down into the depths of your secrets, to go down to the depths of your pain is a scary business, as anybody who's been through psychoanalysis can tell you.

You can never be sure you're going to find a pearl in the depths; you find monsters in the depths. But it seems to me that what you do find in the depths is yourself and each other, and even God is present, there in the depths as well as in the heights. Maybe that's part of what it means to say he descended into hell—"Crucified, died, and was buried, he descended into hell"—Christ is also in hell; and when we're in hell (if we recognize we're in hell) we may find him also there.

■ ■ ■

PAIN AND THE CRAZY, HOLY GRACE OF GOD

Trading with your pain. Pain is treasure. Pain is horror. Pain is that which tempts you like Christ on the cross to say, "My God, my God, why did you abandon me?" Pain is negation of everything that seems precious. But pain also is treasure. And it seems to me so significant that we can come together in places where there is a sense of safety. And, as we come together and try to give each other the most precious thing we have to give because in some sense or another we love each other, what we give each other again and again is our pain. The most precious thing I have to tell you about is the sadness. You don't have to talk about pain, but you have to live out of your pain. Speak out of your depths. Speak out of who you truly are. And when somebody says, "How are you?" don't say, "I'm fine." Maybe just say, "Well, I'm not so good. How are you?" Then let the conversation move. Talk not *about* it, but talk *out of* it. And, I mean, literally talk in this place.

I think of the little boy with the keys in his hand under the pillow and the covers over his head. If only I had been able to raise the covers and say to my father, "I'm scared. I'm scared." Maybe it would've been possible for my father to say, "So am I." And who knows how that might have changed the day? The importance of being able to talk and live out of your pain, the extraordinary importance of that, of pain becoming treasure . . . that's why I think that the other two good and faithful servants were rewarded. The reward is not so much something that God gives them because they did it right, but that in trading with their lives, they truly lived their lives, and ultimately their reward, as the master says, "is to enter into the joy of your master."

Joy is the end of it. Through the gates of pain we enter into joy.

CHAPTER 2

A CRAZY, HOLY GRACE

On a Saturday in late fall, my brother Jamie and I woke up around sunrise. I was ten and he not quite eight, and once we were awake, there was no going back to sleep again because immediately all the excitement of the day that was about to begin burst in upon us like the sun itself, and we could not conceivably have closed our eyes on it. Our mother and father were going to take us to a football game, and although we were not particularly interested in the game, we were desperately interested in being taken. Grandma Buechner had come down from the city to go with us and was asleep in another room. Our parents presumably were also asleep, and so was the couple who worked for us, downstairs in a room off the kitchen. It was much too early to get up, so just as on Christmas morning when you wake up too early to start opening the presents, we amused ourselves as best we could till the rest of the house got moving and it came time to start opening the present of this new and most promising day. We had a roulette wheel, of all things, black and glittery with a chromium spindle at the hub, which it took only the slightest twirl to set spinning and the little ball skittering clickety-click around the rim until the wheel slowed down enough for it to settle into one of the niches and ride out the rest of the spin in silence.

We had a green felt cloth with the numbers and colors marked on it and a box of red, white, and blue poker chips; and all of this we had spread out on the foot of one of our beds, playing with it, when something happened that at the moment neither of us more than half noticed because it was such an ordinary thing in a way, set next to all the extraordinary things that we had reason to believe were going to happen as soon as the day got going. What happened was that our bedroom door opened a little, and somebody looked in on us. It was our father. Later on, we could not remember anything more about it than that, even when we finally got around to pooling our memories of it, which was not until many years later.

If he said anything to us, or if we said anything to him, we neither of us have ever been able to remember it. He could have been either dressed or still in his pajamas for all we noticed. There was apparently nothing about his appearance or about what he said or did that made us look twice at him. There was nothing to suggest that he opened the door for any reason other than just to check on us as he passed by on his way to the bathroom or wherever else we might have thought he was going that early on a Saturday morning, if either of us had bothered to think about it at all. I have no idea how long he stood there looking at us. A few seconds? A few minutes? Did he smile, make a face, wave his hand? I have no idea. All I know is that after a while, he disappeared, closing the door behind him, and we went on playing with our wheel as I assume we had kept on playing with it right along because there was nothing our father had said or done or seemed to want that made us stop. *Clickety clickety click.* Now this number, now that. On one spin we could be rich as Croesus. On the next we could lose our shirts.

How long it was from the moment he closed that door to the moment we opened it, I no longer have any way of knowing, but the interlude can stand in a way for my whole childhood up till then and for everybody else's too, I suppose: childhood as a waiting for you do not know just what and living, as you live in dreams, with little or no sense of sequence or consequence or measurable time. And that moment was also the last of my childhood because, when I opened the door again, measurable time was, among other things, what I opened it on. The click of the latch as I turned the knob was the first tick of the clock that measures everything into before and after, and at that exact moment my once-below-a-time ended and my once-upon-a-time began. From that moment to this I have ridden on time's back as a man rides a horse, knowing fully that the day will come when my ride will end and my time will end and all that I am and all that I have will end with them. Up till then the house had been still. Then, muffled by the closed door, there was a shout from downstairs. It was the husband of the couple who worked for us. His voice was fruity and hollow with something I had never heard in it before. I opened the door.

All over the house doors opened, upstairs and down. My grandmother loomed fierce and terrified in the hallway, her nightgown billowing around her, white and stiff as a sail, her hair down her back. There was a blue haze in the air, faintly bitter and stifling. In what I remember still as a kind of crazy parody of excitement, I grabbed hold of the newel post at the top of the stairs and swung myself around it. "Something terrible has happened!" my grandmother said. She told us to go back to our room. We went back. We looked out the window.

Down below was the gravel drive, the garage with its doors flung wide open and the same blue haze thick inside it and drifting out into the crisp autumn day. I had the sense that my brother and I were looking down from a height many times greater than just the height of the second story of our house. In gray slacks and a maroon sweater, our father was lying in the driveway on his back. By now my mother and grandmother were with him, both in their nightgowns still, barefoot, their hair uncombed. Each had taken one of his legs and was working it up and down like the handle of a pump, but whatever this was supposed to accomplish, it accomplished nothing as far as we could see. A few neighbors had gathered at the upper end of the drive, and my brother and I were there with them, neither knowing how we got there nor daring to go any farther.

Nobody spoke. A car careened up and braked sharp with a spray of gravel. A doctor got out. He was wearing a fedora and glasses. He ran down the driveway with his bag in his hand. He knelt. I remember the man who had roused us sitting somewhere with his head in his hands. I remember the dachshund we had wagging his tail. After a time the doctor came back up the drive, his tread noisy on the gravel. The question the neighbors asked him they asked without words, and without a word the doctor answered them. He barely shook his head. It was not for several days that a note was found. It was written in pencil on the last page of *Gone with the Wind*, which had been published that year, 1936, and it was addressed to my mother. "I adore and love you," it said, "and am no good. . . . Give Freddy my watch. Give Jamie my pearl pin. I give you all my love."

■ ■ ■

God speaks to us through our lives, we often too easily say. *Something* speaks anyway, spells out some sort of godly or godforsaken meaning to us through the alphabet of our years, but often it takes many years and many further spellings out before we start to glimpse, or think we do, a little of what that meaning is. Even then we glimpse it only dimly, like the first trace of dawn on the rim of night, and even then it is a meaning that we cannot fix and be sure of once and for all because it is always incarnate meaning and thus as alive and changing as we are ourselves alive and changing.

A child takes life as it comes because he has no other way of taking it. The world had come to an end that Saturday morning, but each time we had moved to another place, I had seen a world come to an end, and there had always been another world to replace it. When somebody you love dies, Mark Twain said, it is like when your house burns down; it isn't for years that you realize the full extent of your loss. For me it was longer than for most, if indeed I have realized it fully even yet, and in the meanwhile the loss came to get buried so deep in me that after a time I scarcely ever took it out to look at it at all, let alone to speak of it. If ever anybody asked me how my father died, I would say heart trouble. That seemed at least a version of the truth. He had had a heart. It had been troubled. I remembered how his laughter toward the end had rung like a cracked bell. I remembered how when he opened the bedroom door, he had not said good-bye to us in any way that we understood. I remembered what he had written on the last page of the book he had been reading.

And then by grace or by luck, I stopped remembering so completely that when, a year or so later, I came upon my brother crying one day all by himself in his room, I was stopped dead in my tracks. Why was he crying? When I prodded him into telling me that he was crying about something that he would not name but said only had happened a long time ago, I finally knew what he meant, and I can recapture still my astonishment that, for him, a wound was still open that for me, or so I thought, had long since closed. And in addition to the astonishment, there was also a shadow of guilt. It was guilt not only that I had no tears like his to cry with, but that if, no less than he, I had also lost more than I yet knew. I had also, although admittedly at an exorbitant price, made a sort of giddy, tragic, but quite measurable little gain. While my father lived, I was the heir apparent, the crown prince. Now I was not only king, but king in a place that, except for his death, I would probably never have known except in dreams. What I mean is that the place we moved to soon after he died—and it was there that my brother cried, in a house the color of smoked salmon overhanging a harbor of turquoise and ultramarine—was the Land of Oz.

■ ■ ■

No place I have ever been to since—no matter how remote, no matter how strange and lovely—can match the loveliness of the Bermuda islands as they still existed when I first saw them. There were no cars there in those days, none of the sounds or smells of combustion engines of any kind, which have become so much a part of the world we live in that it is hardly possible any more to imagine either the world or our lives without them. The world was quieter and statelier without them, the distances greener and greater. There were only horses and carriages there then—Victorias mostly with their hooded, perambulator tops that could be put up if it rained, and slim English bicycles with bells and baskets, and a narrow-gauge Toonerville Trolley of a railway with wicker armchairs for seats that rattled through pawpaws and banana palms, over high trestles that swayed in the wind across inlets and coves from one end of the fishhook-shaped island to the other no faster, it seemed, than a boy could run. There were fields of lilies, hedges of oleander and hibiscus, passion flowers, moonflowers, and always the small, bent cedars that grew everywhere and whose fragrance enchanted the air you breathed together with the fragrance of horses, the sea, the faint sweetness of kerosene that Bermudians burned in those days when the evenings turned cool.

The houses were sky blue and rose, lemon yellow and lavender and pastel green, all with their blinding white roofs stepped to catch the rain because rain was all the water there was in Bermuda. You drank rain. You bathed in rain. You watched rain move in slow, sad curtains across the harbor where our house was, heard the soft hiss of its advance. It would come up out of nowhere and stop as suddenly, the porous coral roads drying in minutes—the chalky, damp smell of their drying. There were pale pink coral beaches turning to amber in the shallows, then shading off into Gulf Stream greens and purples and deep-sea blue. There were angel fish off our terrace, goggle-eyed squirrel fish, and sergeant majors, striped bumblebee yellow and black. There was a small, battered ferry called *The Dragon* that chugged you across to Hamilton for sixpence with its stern almost awash under a load of bikes. There were the great *Monarch* and the great *Queen*, which on alternate weeks slipped silent as ghosts through the narrows at daybreak, then foghorned, breathy and hoarse, as they started to dock. There was an eccentric with a golden brown beard and hair that grew down to his shoulders who used to hang around the custom sheds with a faraway look in his eyes and was always there by the gangplank when the Furness ships came in, watching the passengers as they got off one by one. Some said that he was looking for a woman who had deserted him, or a lost friend, a lost child, but he himself never told, or even told his name, so Jesus was what people called him because of his long hair and beard, I suppose, or the way he searched all the faces that passed him by. And there were the long-tailed Bermuda gulls.

Grandma Buechner was against our going, and with reason. It was the same kind of extravagance that had so weighed down my father, she said. It was a frivolous place to go at a grave time. It was no place to raise boys. It was escape. "You should stay and face reality," she wrote my mother, and old grandfather Hermann Scharmann, puffing a cigar on Millionaire's Row at Sheepshead Bay, would have nodded agreement if he had not been some fifteen years dead by then and, like his cigar, gone long since to ash. Reality was like the bad weather that you did not put things off because of, or seek refuge from in the Land of Oz. Reality was what the old woman in the joke peered out at through her fingers even though she knew the sight of it might strike her blind.

And my grandmother was right, of course—right in a hundred ways and wrong in as many others. She was right that reality can be harsh and that you shut your eyes to it only at your peril because if you do not face up to the enemy in all his dark power, then the enemy will come up from behind some dark day and destroy you while you are facing the other way. Maybe, if we had stayed home as she did and wept for my father there, we might have become the stronger for it as certainly she became stronger herself because in her chair by the window she stared her doom straight in the eye until somehow she finally managed to stare it down altogether to emerge doom-proof at last with even her mirth intact like the soft, lyric passage that *Götterdämmerung* ends with after all the orchestral *sturm und drang* of Valhalla in flames. Who knows what we might have become? But she was also wrong. *Le bon Dieu*, she would say with that faint little smile, half ironic, half wistful, and if her smile never quite dismissed *le bon Dieu* himself, what I think it did dismiss was anything like the serious possibility that through flaws and fissures in the bedrock harshness of things, there still wells up from time to time, out of a deeper substratum of reality, a kind of crazy, holy grace.

■ ■ ■

"You should stay and face reality," she wrote, and in terms of what was humanly best, this was perhaps the soundest advice she could have given us: that we should stay and, through sheer Scharmann endurance, will, courage, put our lives back together by becoming as strong as she was herself. But when it comes to putting broken lives back together—when it comes, in religious terms, to the saving of souls—the human best tends to be at odds with the holy best. To do for yourself the best that you have it in you to do—to grit your teeth and clench your fists in order to survive the world at its harshest and worst—is, by that very act, to be unable to let something be done for you and in you that is more wonderful still. The trouble with steeling yourself against the harshness of reality is that the same steel that secures your life against being destroyed secures your life also against being opened up and transformed by the holy power that life itself comes from. You can survive on your own. You can grow strong on your own. You can even prevail on your own. But you cannot become human on your own. Surely that is why, in Jesus's sad joke, the rich man has as hard a time getting into Paradise as that camel through the needle's eye because with his credit card in his pocket, the rich man is so effective at getting for himself everything he needs that he does not see that what he needs more than anything else in the world can be had only as a gift. He does not see that the one thing a clenched fist cannot do is accept, even from *le bon Dieu* himself, a helping hand.

My mother took us to Bermuda, of all places, for no motive more profound than simply to get away from things for a while as my grandmother rightly saw; but to get away *from* is also to get away *to*, and that implausible island where we went within a month or two of my father's death turned out to be a place where healing could happen in a way that perhaps would not have been possible anywhere else and to a degree that—even with all the endurance, will, courage we might have been able to muster had we stayed—I do not think we could ever have achieved on our own.

Nazism was on the rise in Germany, and I remember being taken to see the newsreels of Hitler in his glory at the Berlin Olympics. The fall of Austria and the Munich Pact were less than a year away, and the world was bumbling toward war. But all of this was not the world I lived in because, although time had begun for me with the shout from downstairs and the opening of the door, the outward, public history of our times seemed as remote to me then as in many ways it seems to me still. My world was twenty-five miles long, give or take, and some three miles wide at its widest point, and though most of the Americans there were tourists, we were not. We rented a house called The Moorings by the harbor. We settled in and made friends. My brother and I went to a school called Warwick Academy, where we helped drag brushwood to the top of a hill for a bonfire to celebrate the coronation of George the Sixth. All in all it seems to me, looking back, that I lived there with a greater sense of permanence than any place we had lived earlier where there had always been another job in the offing and another house to move to next, and with a sense of the magic and mystery of things greater than I had ever experienced this side of Oz.

There are those who say that William Shakespeare may have had Bermuda in mind when he wrote *The Tempest*, and that is perhaps part of why there are lines from that play that have haunted me all my life and speak better than anything else I know for the spell that island cast. It is a speech of Caliban's:

> Be not affeard, the Isle is full of noyses,
> Sounds, and sweet aires, that give delight and hurt not:
> Sometimes a thousand twangling Instruments
> Will hum about mine eares; and sometime voices,
> That if I then had wak'd after long sleepe,
> Will make me sleepe again, and then in dreaming,
> The clouds methought would open, and shew riches
> Ready to drop upon me, that when I wak'd
> I cried to dream again.

Be not affeard—maybe that was at the heart of it for me. With the worst having happened, there was no longer the worst to fear. Full fathom five my father lay, and part of the riches that dropped on me was the gift of forgetting him. We never really forget anything, they say, and all our pasts lie fathoms deep in us somewhere waiting for some stray sight or smell or scrap of sound to bring them to the surface again. But for the time at least, I let him go as completely as he had let go of us, and the space and peace of that were not the least of the gifts that the island gave.

■ ■ ■

And there were other gifts, too—sounds and sweet airs that gave delight and hurt not. Why I should have remembered it all these years, I can only guess, but one of them was a scene that can have lasted only a moment or two as I was wheeling my bicycle up a steep dirt lane. I have the impression of late afternoon sun and of dust in the air that the sun turned gold, of slowness and stillness and deepest privacy. I see shafts of sun aslant through palm leaves and the flaking plaster of a church rinsed in light back up the hill a way. Through the haze I see a priest come walking down toward me. He is dressed all in black with black gaiters and a low-crowned, broad-brimmed black hat like a priest out of Jane Austen or Laurence Sterne. I remember how out of place he looked, so dark and unyielding in all that unkempt greenness, and yet how much the place seemed somehow his. He passed me by without a word or a nod, he going his way, I going mine, and that was all. The golden air. The purposeful, dark figure passing by like a shadow or a foreshadowing. The sense of another time that I will carry with me to the end of my time.

I remember another much steeper hill that Jamie and I had to climb when we rode our bikes to the beach from school, and how when we got to the top of it, there, suddenly, was the unutterable, blinding blue-green flash of the ocean a mile or so away, and how in a single vast coast we would swoop down on it like birds. I remember a stout, hot-tempered Englishman named Mr. Sutton, who taught at Warwick Academy, and how he lit cigarettes with sun through a magnifying glass and called the two-by-four that he whacked you with if you misbehaved "Sutton's pink pills for pale people." There were flat, sweet yellow buns that you could buy across the street. There were the kites that on Good Friday, for some reason, all the boys in the school went out in the fields to fly, and when you had coaxed your kite high enough, the whole great bellying length of string would start to hum like a thousand twangling instruments about your ears.

There were gifts like these—sights and sounds and smells that I had never known before, staggering in their newness, and there were also gifts I had been born with that the years in Bermuda gave me again in a way to make them seem new. My maternal grandmother, Naya, for instance, came to stay with us for a while, the same old Naya I had served cold string beans to at the age of six, who had given me my taste for books and language and green salad and French, who for years had been teaching me my forebears like irregular verbs—the eccentric New England uncles and the miserly Swiss aunts who roistered through the Gilbert and Sullivan of their endless patter songs. She was the same, but I saw her new—saw her un-booked, un-Pittsburghed, as unhitched from her accustomed world as I was unhitched from mine so that we could meet again as if almost for the first time, like strangers taking shelter from the rain. She drank rum swizzles on the balcony at the 21 Club. In flat-heeled shoes she walked coral roads by the mile. Down at the Furness Line docks once she accidentally set a heavy luggage cart rolling forward by sitting on it, and when my mother came to find us, what she found was Naya in her pearls and a beret held fast by a jet pin pitched like a stevedore to the task of helping my bare-legged brother and me wheel it back to where it belonged, and we laughed till the tears rolled down. I saw us ourselves for the first time as no less wondrously freakish than our freakish forebears had been, the creators of our own new legends.

And Grandma Buechner came too—like the Inspector General, we feared—came to run her white-gloved finger over the upper edges and lower sills of our lives, checking for unreality and extravagance, came to dust off a Scharmann maxim or two. I picture her stout figure looking down from the deck of the *Monarch* to see if she could spot us on the quay below to welcome her. I see her face—half Queen Victoria, half Gertrude Stein—with a sky full of gulls wheeling behind it. I hear her heavy, effortful tread in the hall of what was surely the only smoked salmon-colored house whose rent she ever paid. I had known her power all my life but had never before seen it pitted against an island. It was like trying to drive a breath of fresh air with a croquet mallet, like trying to plump the scent of mimosa into shape, and for as long as she was there, the island prevailed. She grew girlish and coy under the blandishments of the courtly men my mother presented to her. She breathed deep the cedar-laden, salt-sweet air and was as tipsy on it as the rest of us. But when she got home safe to New York again, she wrote my mother that letter about facing reality with the result that that fall we went back and faced it for a winter in an apartment on 90th Street between Lexington and Park. But when the winter was up, she condoned our going back because in the long run she loved us more even than she loved her principles, I suppose, and it was toward the end of that second and last year in Bermuda that I received what may have been the greatest of the gifts the island gave, without any clear idea what it was that I was receiving or that anybody had ever received the likes of before.

■ ■ ■

She was a girl, going on thirteen as I was, with a mouth that turned up at the corners. If we ever spoke to each other about anything of consequence, I have long since forgotten it. I have forgotten the color of her eyes. I have forgotten the sound of her voice. But one day at dusk we were sitting side by side on a crumbling stone wall watching the Salt Kettle ferries come and go when, no less innocently than the time I reached up to the bust of Venus under my grandfather's raffish gaze, our bare knees happened to touch for a moment, and in that moment I was filled with such a sweet panic and anguish of longing for I had no idea what that I knew my life could never be complete until I found it. "Difference of sex no more we knew / Than our guardian angels do," as John Donne wrote, and in the ordinary sense of the word, no love could have been less erotic, but it was the Heavenly Eros in all its glory nonetheless—there is no question about that. It was the upward-reaching and fathomlessly hungering, heartbreaking love for the beauty of the world at its most beautiful, and, beyond that, for that beauty east of the sun and west of the moon, which is past the reach of all but our most desperate desiring and is finally the beauty of Beauty itself, of Being itself and what lies at the heart of Being.

Like all children I had been brought up till then primarily on the receiving end of love. My parents loved me, my grandparents, a handful of others maybe, and I had accepted their love the way a child does, as part of the givenness of things, and responded to it the way a cat purrs when you pat it. But now for the first time I was myself the source and giver of a love so full to overflowing that I could not possibly have expressed it to that girl whose mouth turned up at the corners even if I had had the courage to try. And let anyone who dismisses such feelings as puppy love, silly love, be set straight because I suspect that rarely if ever again in our lives does Eros touch us in such a distilled and potent form as when we are children and have so little else in our hearts to dilute it. I loved her more than I knew how to say even to myself. Whether in any way she loved me in return, I neither knew nor, as far as I can remember, was even especially concerned to find out. Just to love her was all that I asked. Eros itself, even tinged with the sadness of knowing that I could never fully find on earth or sea whatever it was that I longed for, was gift enough.

Then, as unforeseeably as it had begun, it ended. On the first of September, Hitler's armies invaded Poland, and on the third, England and France declared war on Germany. The rumor soon spread that the Germans had plans to capture Bermuda for a submarine base, and all Americans were required to leave. It happened very suddenly, and in the haste and confusion of it, I never even knew when she left or had a chance to say good-bye. The *Monarch* and the *Queen* were painted gray for camouflage, and on the *Queen*, I think, with the portholes blacked out and no one allowed so much as to light a match on deck after dark, we set sail for a reality that we were forced, with the rest of the world, to face at last.

■ ■ ■

Whatever reality is. Reality is what is, I suppose, is whatever there is that seems real; and since what seems real to one need not seem real to another—like color to the blind, like hope to the hopeless—we all create our own realities as we go along. Reality for me was this. Out of my father's death there came, for me, a new and, in many ways, happier life. The shock of his death faded and so did those feelings about it that led me for a while to speak of it in terms of heart trouble, because the word *suicide* seemed somehow shameful and better left unspoken. I cannot say the grief faded because, in a sense, I had not yet, unlike my brother, really felt that grief. That was not to happen for thirty years or more. But the grief was postponed, allowed to sink beneath the whole bright accumulation of the Bermuda years, and for many more years. Only in my middle age did it become real enough for me to weep real tears at last and to see better than I ever had earlier who it was that I was weeping for and who I was that was weeping. In that Never Never Land, that Oz of an island, where we had no roots, I found for the first time a sense of being rooted. In that land where as foreigners we could never really belong, I found a sense of belonging. In that most frivolous place that the travel brochures billed as the vacationers' paradise, I made what was perhaps the least frivolous discovery that I had made up till then, which was that love is not merely a warmth to bask in the way the boatloads of honeymooners basked in the warmth of Coral Beach but a grave, fierce yearning and reaching out for Paradise itself, a losing and finding of the self in the Paradise of another. This is the reality of those years as I look back at them, and part of their reality for me is that all the healing and strengthening that came my way then came my way largely as a gift, and as a gift that implies a giver. Did it?

There are other ways of looking at those years, of course. The commonsense way would be to say simply that the boy grew up a little. Time heals all wounds, and his were no exception. Things started to fall in place for him, that's all. What happened happened as much by chance as the chance pattern of raindrops on a windowpane, as much by luck as happening to draw the lucky number in a raffle. If you want to speak in terms of a gift and a giver, then you should speak of the boy's grandmother, that formidable old lady who seems to have gotten short shrift in this account, but who paid the rent after all and financed the whole operation even though it was against her better judgment to do so. Or there could be psychological ways. You could say that the trauma of the father's suicide was such that the boy, unable to come to terms with his own feelings, repressed them to the extent that they were bound to cause psychological problems later on. You could speak in terms of Oedipal conflict and say that part of the reason the boy seemed to recover from his grief as quickly as he did was that, with his father's death, he got what, subconsciously, he had, of course, always wanted, which was his mother to himself. And you could say that one consequence of that might well have been just such a residue of anxiety and guilt as might in later years lead him to seek consolation in religious fantasy, to dream up for himself a father in Heaven to replace the one he had lost. As for the incident of the girl, it was clearly a case of adolescent sexuality romanticized to the level of a temporary obsession.

I cannot deny such ways of looking at those years, nor do I want to. These and many other such insights seem real to me. Yes, time heals all wounds or at least dresses them, makes them endurable. Yes, at the king's death, the grief of the prince is mitigated by becoming king himself. Yes, the great transfiguring power of sex stirs early and seismically in all of us. Which of us can look at our own religion or lack of it without seeing in it the elements of wish-fulfillment? Which of us can look back at our own lives without seeing in them the role of blind chance and dumb luck? But faith, says the author of the Epistle to the Hebrews, is "the assurance of things hoped for, the conviction of things not seen," and looking back at those distant years I choose not to deny, either, the compelling sense of an unseen giver and a series of hidden gifts as not only another part of their reality, but the deepest part of all.

* * *

My grandmother might have been right about our going to
Bermuda. It could have been a terrible mistake. Instead maybe
it was the best thing we ever did. My father's death could have
closed doors in me once and for all against the possibility of ever
giving entrance to such love and thereby to such pain again.
Instead, it opened up some door in me to the pain of others—
not that I did much about the others, God knows, or have ever
done much about them since I am too lily-livered for that, too
weak of faith, too self-absorbed and squeamish—but such pain
as I had known in my own life opened up, if not my hands to
help much, at least my eyes to begin seeing anyway that there is
pain in every life, even the apparently luckiest, that buried griefs
and hurtful memories are part of us all. And there was so much
else to see too—the priest in his black gaiters, the pull and hum
of the Good Friday kites, the girl sitting beside me on the wall
at Salt Kettle—and there is so much to see always, things too
big to take in all at once, things so small as hardly to be noticed.
And though they may well come by accident, these moments of
our seeing, I choose to believe that it is by no means by accident
when they open our hearts as well as our eyes.

A crazy, holy grace I have called it. Crazy because whoever
could have predicted it? Who can ever foresee the crazy how
and when and where of a grace that wells up out of the lostness
and pain of the world and of our own inner worlds? And holy
because these moments of grace come ultimately from farther
away than Oz and deeper down than doom, holy because they
heal and hallow. "For all thy blessings, known and unknown,
remembered and forgotten, we give thee thanks," runs an old
prayer, and it is for the all but unknown ones and the more

than half-forgotten ones that we do well to look back over the journeys of our lives because it is their presence that makes the life of each of us a sacred journey. We have a hard time seeing such blessed and blessing moments as the gifts I choose to believe they are and a harder time still reaching out toward the hope of a giving hand, but part of the gift is to be able, at least from time to time, to be assured and convinced without seeing, as Hebrews says, because that is of the very style and substance of faith as well as what drives it always to seek a farther and a deeper seeing still.

There will always be some who say that such faith is only a dream, and God knows there is none who can say it more devastatingly than we sometimes say it to ourselves, but if so, I think of it as like the dream that Caliban dreamed. Faith is like the dream in which the clouds open to show such riches ready to drop upon us that when we wake into the reality of nothing more than common sense, we cry to dream again because the dreaming seems truer than the waking does to the fullness of reality not as we have seen it, to be sure, but as, by faith, we trust it to be without seeing. Faith is both the dreaming and the crying. Faith is the assurance that the best and holiest dream is true after all. Faith in *something*—if only in the proposition that life is better than death—is what makes our journeys through time bearable. When faith ends, the journey ends—ends either in a death like my father's or in the living death of those who believe themselves to be without hope.[1]

PART 2

THE MAGIC OF MEMORY

CHAPTER 3

A ROOM CALLED REMEMBER

And they brought in the ark of God, and set it inside the tent which David had pitched for it; and they offered burnt offerings and peace offerings before God. . . . Then on that day David first appointed that thanksgiving be sung to the LORD by Asaph and his brethren. "O give thanks to the LORD, call on his name, make known his deeds among the peoples! . . . Glory in his holy name; let the hearts of those who seek the LORD rejoice! Seek the LORD and his strength, seek his presence continually! Remember the wonderful works that he has done, the wonders he wrought, the judgments he uttered."

1 CHRONICLES 16:1, 7–9, 10–12

And he said, "Jesus, remember me when you come into your kingdom power." And he said to him, "Truly, I say to you, today you will be with me in Paradise."

LUKE 23:42–43

Every once in a while, if you're like me, you have a dream that wakes you up. Sometimes it's a bad dream—a dream in which the shadows become so menacing that your heart skips a beat and you come awake to the knowledge that not even the actual darkness of night is as fearsome as the dreamed darkness, not even the shadows without as formidable as the shadows within. Sometimes it's a sad dream—a dream sad enough to bring real tears to your sleeping eyes so that it's your tears that you wake up by, wake up to. Or again, if you're like me, there are dreams that take a turn so absurd that you wake laughing—as if you need to be awake to savor the full richness of the comedy. Rarest of all is the dream that wakes you with what I can only call its truth.

The path of your dream winds now this way, now that—one scene fades into another, people come and go the way they do in dreams—and then suddenly, deep out of wherever it is that dreams come from, something rises up that shakes you to your foundations. The mystery of the dream suddenly lifts like fog, and for an instant it is as if you glimpse a truth truer than any you knew that you knew, if only a truth about yourself. It is too much truth for the dream to hold anyway, and the dream breaks.

Several years ago I had such a dream, and it is still extraordinarily fresh in my mind. I dreamt that I was staying in a hotel somewhere and that the room I was given was a room that I loved. I no longer have any clear picture of what the room looked like, and even in the dream itself I think it wasn't so much the way the room looked that pleased me as it was the way it made me feel. It was a room where I felt happy and at peace, where everything seemed the way it should be and everything about myself seemed the way it should be too. Then, as the dream went on, I wandered off to other places and did other things and finally, after many adventures, ended back at the same hotel again. Only this time I was given a different room, which I didn't feel comfortable in at all. It seemed dark and cramped, and I felt dark and cramped in it. So I made my way down to the man at the desk and told him my problem. On my earlier visit, I said, I'd had this marvelous room that was just right for me in every way and that I'd very much like if possible to have again. The trouble, I explained, was that I hadn't kept track of where the room was and didn't know how to find it or how to ask for it. The clerk was very understanding. He said that he knew exactly the room I meant and that I could have it again anytime I wanted it. All I had to do, he said, was ask for it by its name. So then, of course, I asked him what the name of the room was. He would be happy to tell me, he said, and then he told me. The name of the room, he said, was Remember.

Remember, he said. The name of the room I wanted was Remember. That was what woke me. It shocked me awake, and the shock of it, the dazzling unexpectedness of it, is vivid to me still. I knew it was a good dream, and I felt that in some unfathomable way it was also a true dream. The fact that I did not understand its truth did not keep it from being in some sense also a blessed dream, a healing dream, because you do not need to understand healing to be healed or know anything about blessing to be blessed. The sense of peace that filled me in that room, the knowledge that I could return to it whenever I wanted to or needed to—that was where the healing and blessing came from. And the name of the room—that was where the mystery came from; that was at the heart of the healing, though I did not fully understand why. The name of the room was Remember. *Why* Remember? What was there about remembering that brought a peace so deep, a sense of well-being so complete and intense that it jolted me awake in my bed? It was a dream that seemed true not only for me, but true for everybody. What are we to remember—all of us? To what end and purpose are we to remember?

One way or another, we are always remembering, of course. There is no escaping it even if we want to, or at least no escaping it for long, though God knows there are times when we try to, don't want to remember. In one sense the past is dead and gone, never to be repeated, over and done with, but in another sense, it is, of course, not done with at all or at least not done with us. Every person we have ever known, every place we have ever seen, everything that has ever happened to us—it all lives and breathes deep in us somewhere whether we like it or not, and sometimes it doesn't take much to bring it back to the surface in bits and pieces. A scrap of some song that was popular years ago. A book we read as a child. A stretch of road we used to travel. An old photograph, an old letter. There is no telling what trivial thing may do it, and then suddenly there it all is—something that happened to us once—and it is there not just as a picture on the wall to stand back from and gaze at, but as a reality we are so much a part of still and that is still so much a part of us that we feel with something close to its original intensity and freshness what it felt like, say, to fall in love at the age of sixteen, or to smell the smells and hear the sounds of a house that has long since disappeared, or to laugh till the tears ran down our cheeks with somebody who died more years ago than we can easily count or for whom, in every way that matters, we might as well have died years ago ourselves. Old failures, old hurts. Times too beautiful to tell or too terrible. Memories come at us helter-skelter and unbidden, sometimes so thick and fast that they are more than we can handle in their poignancy, sometimes so sparsely that we all but cry out to remember more.

But the dream seems to say more than that, to speak of a different kind of memory and to speak of remembering in a different kind of way. The kind of memories I have been naming are memories that come and go more or less on their own and apart from any choice of ours. Things remind us, and the power is the things', not ours. The room called Remember, on the other hand, is a room we can enter whenever we like so that the power of remembering becomes our own power. Also, the kind of memories we normally have are memories that stir emotions in us that are as varied as the memories that stir them. The room called Remember, on the other hand, is a room where all emotions are caught up in and transcended by an extraordinary sense of well-being. It is the room of all rooms where we feel at home and at peace. So the question is, what do these differences point to—the difference between the haphazard memories that each day brings to us willy-nilly and the memories represented by the room in the dream.

First of all, I think, they point to remembering as much more of a conscious act of the will than it normally is for us. We are all such escape artists, you and I. We don't like to get too serious about things, especially about ourselves. When we are with other people, we are apt to talk about almost anything under the sun except for what really matters to us, except for our own lives, except for what is going on inside our own skins. We pass the time of day. We chatter. We hold each other at bay, keep our distance from each other even when God knows it is precisely each other that we desperately need.

And it is the same thing when we are alone. Let's say it is late evening and everybody else has gone away or gone to bed.

THE MAGIC OF MEMORY

The time is ripe for looking back over the day, the week, the year, and trying to figure out where we have come from and where we are going to, for sifting through the things we have done and the things we have left undone for a clue to who we are and who, for better or worse, we are becoming. But again and again we avoid the long thoughts. We turn on the television maybe. We pick up a newspaper or a book. We find some chore to do that could easily wait for the next day. We cling to the present out of wariness of the past. We cling to the surface out of fear of what lies beneath the surface. And why not, after all? We get tired. We get confused. We need such escape as we can find. But there is a deeper need yet, I think, and that is the need—not all the time, surely, but from time to time—to enter that still room within us all where the past lives on as part of the present, where the dead are alive again, where we are most alive ourselves to the long journeys of our lives with all their twistings and turnings and to where our journeys have brought us. The name of the room is Remember—the room where with patience, with charity, with quietness of heart, we remember consciously to remember the lives we have lived.

So much has happened to us all over the years. So much has happened within us and through us. We are to take time to remember what we can about it and what we dare. That's what entering the room means, I think. It means taking time to remember on purpose. It means not picking up a book for once or turning on the radio, but letting the mind journey gravely, deliberately, back through the years that have gone by but are not gone. It means a deeper, slower kind of remembering; it means remembering as a searching and finding. The room is there for all of us to enter if we choose to, and the process of entering it is not unlike the process of praying, because praying too is a slow, grave journey—a search to find the truth of our own lives at their deepest and dearest, a search to understand, to hear and be heard.

"Nobody knows the trouble I've seen" goes the old spiritual, and, of course, nobody knows the trouble we have any of us seen—the hurt, the sadness, the bad mistakes, the crippling losses—but we know it. We are to remember it. And the happiness we have seen too—the precious times, the precious people, the moments in our lives when we were better than we know how to be. Nobody knows that either, but we know it. We are to remember it. And then, if my dream was really a true dream, we will find, beyond any feelings of joy or regret that one by one the memories give rise to, a profound and undergirding peace, a sense that in some unfathomable way all is well.

We have survived, you and I. Maybe that is at the heart of our remembering. After twenty years, forty years, sixty years or eighty, we have made it to this year, this day. We needn't have made it. There were times we never thought we would and nearly didn't. There were times we almost hoped we wouldn't, were ready to give the whole thing up. Each must speak for himself, for herself, but I can say for myself that I have seen sorrow and pain enough to turn the heart to stone. Who hasn't? Many times I have chosen the wrong road, or the right road for the wrong reason. Many times I have loved the people I love too much for either their good or mine, and others I might have loved I have missed loving and lost. I have followed too much the devices and desires of my own heart, as the old prayer goes, yet often when my heart called out to me to be brave, to be kind, to be honest, I have not followed at all.

To remember my life is to remember countless times when I might have given up, gone under, when humanly speaking

I might have gotten lost beyond the power of any to find me. But I didn't. I have not given up. And each of you, with all the memories you have and the tales you could tell, you also have not given up. You also are survivors and are here. And what does that tell us, our surviving? It tells us that weak as we are, a strength beyond our strength has pulled us through at least this far, at least to this day. Foolish as we are, a wisdom beyond our wisdom has flickered up just often enough to light us if not to the right path through the forest, at least to a path that leads forward, that is bearable. Faint of heart as we are, a love beyond our power to love has kept our hearts alive.

So in the room called Remember it is possible to find peace—the peace that comes from looking back and remembering to remember that though most of the time we failed to see it, we were never really alone. We could never have made it this far if we had had only each other to depend on, because nobody knows better than we do ourselves the undependability and frailty of even the strongest of us. Who or what was with us all those years? Who or what do we have to thank for our survival? Our lucky stars? Maybe just that. Maybe we have nothing more to thank than that. Our lucky stars.

■ ■ ■

But David the king had more than that, or thought he did. "O give thanks to the LORD," he cried out, "make known his deeds among the peoples!" He had brought the Ark of the Covenant into Jerusalem and placed it in a room, a tent, and to the sound of harp, lyre, cymbals, and trumpet he sang his wild and exultant song. "Remember the wonderful works that he has done," he sang, "the wonders he wrought, the judgments he uttered." *Remember* was the song David sang, and what memories he had or was to have, what a life to remember! His failure as a husband and a father, his lust for Bathsheba and the murder of her husband, his crime against Naboth and the terrible denunciation of the prophet Nathan, his failures, his betrayals, his hypocrisy. But "Tell of his salvation from day to day" (1 Chronicles 16:23), his song continues nonetheless and continued all his life, and I take him to mean not just that the telling was to take place from day to day, but that salvation itself takes place from day to day. Every day, as David remembered, he had been somehow saved—saved enough to survive his own darkness and lostness and folly, saved enough to go on through thick and thin to the next day and the next day's saving and the next. "Remember the wonders he wrought, the judgments he uttered," David cries out in his song, and the place where he remembers these wonders and judgments is his own past in all its brokenness and the past of his people before him, of Abraham, Isaac, and Jacob, the Exodus, the entrance into the Promised Land, which are all part of our past too as Christ also is part of our past, that Exodus, that Promised Land, and all those mightier wonders yet. That's what he remembers and sings out for us all to remember.

"Seek the LORD and his strength, seek his presence continually" goes the song—seek him in the room in the tent where the holy ark is, seek him in the room in the dream. It is the LORD, it is God, who has been with us through all our days and years whether we knew it or not, he sings—with us in our best moments and in our worst moments, to heal us with his wonders, to wound us healingly with his judgments, to bless us in hidden ways though more often than not we had forgotten his name. It is God that David thanks and not his lucky stars. "O give thanks to the LORD . . . make known his deeds among the peoples," he sings; remember and make known the deeds that he wrought among the years of your own lives. Is he right? Was it God? Is it God we have to thank, you and I, for having made it somehow to this day?

Again each of us must speak for himself, for herself. We must, each one of us, remember our own lives. Someone died whom we loved and needed, and from somewhere something came to fill our emptiness and mend us where we were broken. Was it only time that mended, only the resurging busyness of life that filled our emptiness? In anger we said something once that we could have bitten our tongues out for afterward, or in anger somebody said something to us. But out of somewhere forgiveness came, a bridge was rebuilt; or maybe forgiveness never came, and to this day we have found no bridge back. Is the human heart the only source of its own healing? Is it the human conscience only that whispers to us that in bitterness and estrangement is death? We listen to the evening news with its usual recital of shabbiness and horror, and God, if we believe in him at all, seems remote and powerless, a child's dream. But there are other times—often the most unexpected, unlikely times—when strong as life itself comes the sense that there is a holiness deeper than shabbiness and horror and at the very heart of darkness a light unutterable. Is it only the unpredictable fluctuations of the human spirit that we have to thank? We must each of us answer for ourselves, remember for ourselves, preach to ourselves our own sermons. But "Remember the wonderful works," sings King David, because if we remember deeply and truly, he says, we will know whom to thank, and in that room of thanksgiving and remembering there is peace.

Then hope. Then at last we see what hope is and where it comes from, hope as the driving power and outermost edge *human hope*

of faith. Hope stands up to its knees in the past and keeps its eyes on the future. There has never been a time past when God wasn't with us as the strength beyond our strength, the wisdom beyond our wisdom, as whatever it is in our hearts—whether we believe in God or not—that keeps us human enough at least to get by despite everything in our lives that tends to wither the heart and make us less than human. To remember the past is to see that we are here today by grace, that we have survived as a gift.

And what does that mean about the future? What do we have to hope for, you and I? Humanly speaking, we have only the human best to hope for: that we will live out our days in something like peace and the ones we love with us; that if our best dreams are never to come true, neither at least will our worst fears; that something we find to do with our lives will make some little difference for good somewhere; and that when our lives end we will be remembered a little while for the little good we did. That is our human hope. But in the room called Remember we find something beyond it.

"Remember the wonderful works that he has done," goes David's song—remember what he has done in the lives of each of us; and beyond that remember what he has done in the life of the world; remember above all what he has done in Christ— remember those moments in our own lives when with only the dullest understanding but with the sharpest longing we have glimpsed that Christ's kind of life is the only life that matters and that all other kinds of life are riddled with death; remember those moments in our lives when Christ came to us in countless disguises through people who one way or another strengthened us, comforted us, healed us, judged us, by the power of Christ alive within them. All that is the past. All that is what there is to remember. And *because* that is the past, *because* we remember, we have this high and holy hope: that what he has done, he will continue to do, that what he has begun in us and our world, he will in unimaginable ways bring to fullness and fruition.

"Let the sea roar, and all that fills it, let the field exult, and everything in it! Then shall the trees of the wood sing for joy," says David (1 Chronicles 16:32–33). And *shall* is the verb of hope. Then death shall be no more, neither shall there be mourning or crying. Then shall my eyes behold him and not as a stranger. Then his Kingdom shall come at last and his will shall be done in us and through us and for us. Then the trees of the wood shall sing for joy as already they sing a little even now sometimes when the wind is in them, and as underneath their singing our own hearts too already sing a little sometimes at this holy hope we have.

■ ■ ■

The past and the future. Memory and expectation. Remember and hope. Remember and wait. Wait for him whose face we all of us know because somewhere in the past we have faintly seen it, whose life we all of us thirst for because somewhere in the past we have seen it lived, have maybe even had moments of living it ourselves. Remember him who himself remembers us as he promised to remember the thief who died beside him. To have faith is to remember and wait, and to wait in hope is to have what we hope for already begin to come true in us through our hoping. Praise him.[2]

CHAPTER 4

THE MAGIC
OF MEMORY

I bring Naya into the Magic Kingdom. Naya is my grand-mother, my mother's mother, who died in 1961 in her ninety-fourth year. She walks across the green library carpet and stands at the window looking out across the stream toward my wife's vegetable garden and the rising meadow behind it with a dirt track running through it up into the sugar woods on the hillside.

The Magic Kingdom is my haven and sanctuary, the place where I do my work, the place of my dreams and of my dreaming. I originally named it the Magic Kingdom as a kind of joke—part Disneyland, part the Land of Oz—but by now it has become simply its name. It consists of the small room you enter through, where the family archives are, the office, where my desk and writing paraphernalia are, and the library, which is by far the largest room of the three. Its walls are lined with ceiling-high shelves except where the windows are, and it is divided roughly in half by shoulder-high shelves that jut out at right angles from the others but with an eight-foot space between them so that it is still one long room despite the dividers. There are such wonderful books in it that I expect people to tremble with excitement, as I would, on entering it for the first time, but few of them do so because they don't know or care enough about books to have any idea what they are seeing.

They are the books I have been collecting all my life, beginning with the Uncle Wiggily series by Howard R. Garis. In 1932, when I was six, I sent my unfortunate mother all over Washington, D.C., looking for *Uncle Wiggily's Ice Cream Party*, but she never found it, and it wasn't until about sixty years later that I finally located a copy and completed the set. There are first editions of all the Oz books, some of them the same copies I read as a child, with "Frebby Buechner" scrawled in them because I was less sure about the difference between *b*'s and *d*'s in those days than I have become since, and also of both *Alice in Wonderland* and *Alice Through the Looking Glass*, with a later edition of each signed by the original Alice herself when she came to this country in 1932 as an old lady to receive an honorary doctorate from Columbia University on the centenary of Lewis Carroll's birth. Underneath her academic robes she wore a corsage of roses and lilies of the valley and in her acceptance speech said she would prize the honor "for the rest of my days, which may not be very long." She died in 1934 at the age of eighty-two. There is a drab little Jenny Wren of Dickens's *A Christmas Carol* as first published in 1843 with green endpapers and the four hand-colored, steel-engraved plates by John Leech, and a *Moby-Dick; or, The Whale* in the original shabby purple-brown cloth with the "usual moderate foxing" throughout, as the catalogue description apologetically notes. There are a number of seventeenth-century folios, including the sermons of Lancelot Andrewes, Jeremy Taylor, and John Donne, that I started buying when my wife and I were on our honeymoon in England in 1956 with some British royalties that were due me then. There is North's *Plutarch* and Florio's

Montaigne and the first collected edition of Ben Jonson, 1692, which I was beside myself with excitement to discover bore the inscription *Jo: Swift, Coli Nova* in an eighteenth-century hand, only to learn from the British Museum years later that it was not, as I'd wildly hoped, the great Jonathan but one John Swift, who matriculated at New College, Oxford, at the age of fifteen.

On the walls are the framed autographs of some of my heroes. There is a photograph of the portrait of Henry James that his friend Sargent painted on the occasion of his seventieth birthday, inscribed by both Sargent and the Master himself, who distributed prints of it to the faithful. Nearby Anthony Trollope has signed his name together with the words "Very faithfully" beneath a *carte de visite* photograph that shows him in granny glasses scowling through whiskers that erupt from his face like the stuffing of an old sofa—"all gobble and glare," as Henry James once described him in a letter—and there is a sepia cabinet photograph of Mark Twain on the lower margin of which he has written, "It is your human environment that makes climate," whatever exactly he meant by that. And then, matted with red damask in a gilt frame, there is the upper part of a sixteenth-century vellum document in which Queen Elizabeth, the only *real* Queen Elizabeth, grants permission to someone whose name I cannot make out to travel to Flanders on official business. When the trip was completed, the document was canceled with four gill-like incisions, and at the top of the page the queen signed it "Elizabeth R." Between her signature and the document's first line there are two free-floating squiggles, which my wife and I long ago decided mark where she tried out her quill pen to make sure it wouldn't spatter ink when she made the great flowing loops that fly out like pennants in the wind from the bottom of the *E* and *Z* and *R* and the upper staff of the *b*.

On the sash of the large window at the end of the room, where Naya stands waiting for me to get on with my description, there is a stone I found wedged into a crack in the rocky ledge we stepped ashore on when I made a pilgrimage to the island of Outer Fame in the North Sea one summer in honor of St. Godric, who often visited there in his seafaring days in the twelfth century and about whom I had written a novel several years earlier. In the novel I describe how on his first visit to the island Godric ran into St. Cuthbert, who had died some four hundred years before. Cuthbert says that long before Godric arrived, he was expected there and then explains himself by saying, "When a man leaves home, he leaves behind some scrap of his heart. Is it not so, Godric? . . . It's the same with a place a man is going to. Only then he sends a scrap of his heart ahead." When I finally managed to pry the stone loose with my pocketknife, I discovered, to my wonderment, that it was unmistakably heart-shaped, and I have fastened Cuthbert's explanation to the back of it with Scotch tape. On top of one of the divider bookshelves is a Rogers Group that depicts King Lear awakening from his madness in the presence of his old friend Kent, disguised as a servant, and the Doctor, and Cordelia, whose forehead he is reaching out to touch as he says, in the words inscribed on the statue's base, "You are a spirit, I know. When did you die?" On the windowsill stands the bronze head of my childhood friend, the poet James Merrill, sculpted in the summer of 1948, when we shared a house on Georgetown Island in Maine while he worked on his *First Poems* and I on *A Long Day's Dying*, which was my first novel. I remember feeling rather miffed that it was Jimmy rather than I whom our friend Morris Levine had chosen to immortalize, but I got over it.

Naya is sitting in the wing chair by the window looking as

she did when she was in her late eighties. Her "eyes mid many wrinkles, her eyes," her "ancient, glittering eyes, are gay," as Yeats wrote of the old Chinese men in "Lapis Lazuli." Her hair is in a loose bun held together by several tortoise-shell pins, and there are a few stray wisps floating free. She is wearing a black dress with a diamond bar pin. One hand extends out over the arm of the chair, palm upward, and she lightly rubs her thumb and middle finger together with a circular motion, as she often did when she was waiting for something to happen.

"Jimmy was a spirit I knew," she says. "When did he die?"

He died on February 6, 1995, and on the day before, from a hospital in Arizona, he apparently made three phone calls— one to his mother, one to his former psychiatrist, Dr. Detre, and one to me. He was having some difficulty breathing, but otherwise sounded entirely himself. He said he was glad that whatever was happening to him was happening far from home where he wouldn't be "smothered with concern," as he put it. He said that he was in no serious pain and that when they had given him some Welch's grape juice sorbet earlier in the day, it had tasted so good to him he had asked for another. He asked me to stay in touch with his mother and sent his love to my wife. I told him I would say some powerful prayers for him, and he said, "That is exactly what I want you to do." He called me "my dearest friend," which I couldn't remember his ever having done before, and when I phoned the next morning to find out how things were going with him, I was told that he had died a few hours earlier. It was only then that I realized that the purpose of his call had, of course, been to say good-bye, and ever since then the ground I stand on has felt less sure and solid beneath my feet.

"The poor lad," Naya says. "I remember how he used to

come spend weekend passes with us in Tryon when he was in basic training at Camp Croft during the war. He sometimes played Mozart for us on that awful upright that came with the dark little cabin we were renting that year, his glasses perpetually sliding down the bridge of his nose. We talked about Proust and Elinor Wylie, and your Uncle George Wick listened to him as though he was a visitor from Mars and plied him with daiquiris till he couldn't see straight. Was there ever anybody *en ce bas monde* who was less cut out to be a GI?"

"He wrote me about a terrible march he was on once during infantry training," I tell her. "It was blistering hot, and they were all loaded down with full field packs and steel helmets and bayonets fixed to their M-1 rifles. There was a grubby-faced little girl standing barefoot by the side of the red-clay road to watch, and he said that as he passed by in front of her, she handed him a peach and he burst into tears."

Naya takes a Chesterfield out of her knitting bag and places it dead center between her lips. I had forgotten all about her formidable Zippo lighter until she opens it with a metallic clink and produces a raw whiff of lighter fluid and a towering flame. Skeins of smoke drift around her head in the sunlit air as she recites, "I did but see her passing by, yet will I love her till I die."

"Can you really be there, my dearest dear, or am I only dreaming you?" I say. She narrows her eyes at me, smiling faintly, and gives me her riverboat-gambler look.[3]

■ ■ ■

The answer to my question is that yes, Naya can really be there. I suspect there is no one on earth, or anywhere else, who cannot really be there if I want them to be and summon them properly.

"I think about dying a lot these days," I say to her. "I think about how much time I've got left. Sometimes they're sad thoughts, but not always. Sometimes the sadness is lost in wondering what will come next. If anything comes."[4]

■ ■ ■

Naya is knitting a sock and has her knitting face on—her eyebrows slightly raised, her lips pressed tight.

"You've already set sail," I say. "What can you tell me about it?"

She glances at me over the top of her spectacles and lets her needles come to rest.

"My poor, ignorant boy," she says, "don't you know better than to ask a question like that when I'm turning a heel?"

The ball of wool falls off her lap and rolls toward me across the green carpet. I pick it up and put it on her lap again.

She says, "When somebody once asked your Uncle Jim if some friend or other had passed away, he answered in his inimitable fashion by saying, 'Passed away? Good God, he's dead,' and I know just how he felt. I always thought 'passed away' was a silly way of putting it, like calling the water closet a powder room—or calling it a water closet for that matter—and I am here to tell you that it is also very misleading."

She says, "It is the *world* that passes away," and flutters one hand delicately through the air to show the manner of its passing. Her sapphire ring glitters in the sun.

"When I used to lie there in that shadowy little room Mrs. Royal gave me in her establishment that looked out onto the garden, with your blessed mother or Ruth dropping by every day or so to keep me abreast of the local gossip at Missildine's, where everybody used to congregate for a Coke after picking up the mail and Miss Capps would read the picture postcards over your shoulder, I could feel the world gradually slowing down more and more until one night, after that charming nurse whose name I regret to say I've forgotten turned out the light and was getting ready to go home, I realized it was finally slow enough for me to get off, and that is just what I proceeded to do. It was rather like getting off a streetcar before it has quite come to a stop—a little jolt when my foot first struck the pavement, and then the world clanged its bell and went rattling off down the tracks without me. Myrtle, that was her name unfortunately, but what a comfort she was."

She closes her eyes and is silent while she tries to summon up the scrap of poetry she is after. Then with one slender finger she taps out the meter on the arm of her chair as she recites it with her eyes still closed.

"And when like her, oh Saki, you shall pass
Among the Guests Star-scatter'd on the Grass,
And in your joyous errand reach the spot
Where I made One—turn down an empty Glass.

"A lovely, sad thought," she says, "but for me there really wasn't any sadness. I felt nothing so much as astonishment. I had lived so many years by then that I was sure the only thing that could ever finish me off would be a violent death of some kind—a smashup on that corkscrew road to Asheville perhaps, or a bolt of lightning. So then when it finally happened right there in my bed with the night light on and that nice nurse standing by, nothing could have been more peaceful, and I was astonished."

"I was sitting upstairs at my desk in Exeter when I got the news," I say, "and I remember leaning forward and resting my head on top of the typewriter and seeing my tears trickle down into the keys."

"That was a fitting tribute from a young man of literary aspirations," she says.

I say, "That was almost forty years ago, and I doubt if a single day has gone by without my missing you."

"Ours was a marriage made in Heaven," she says. "I loved to talk, and you loved to listen. Even when you were a little boy in a red beret, you would sit there with your eyes round as saucers while I rattled on."

"Tell me about wherever you are now," I say. "Rattle on about what it's like to be dead."

■ ■ ■

My mother, the elder of Naya's two daughters, refused to talk about death the way she refused to talk about a great many other things. I remember telling her once that unless she started balancing her checkbook, she would go on overdrawing her account with disastrous results for the rest of eternity, and before I had much more than begun my lecture, she clapped her hands over her ears so she couldn't hear a syllable. She refused even to talk about people she loved who had died— Naya, for instance. It made her too sad, she said. Her New York apartment was full of photographs in silver frames, leather frames, Victorian rhinestone and millefiori frames, but they were photographs only of the living. Once in Vermont when I showed her a picture that I had dug up somewhere of her father as a young man, she hardly so much as glanced at it.

But there was one day, I remember, when in the midst of some conversation we were having about nothing in particular she suddenly turned to me and said out of the blue, "Do you *death*

really believe anything *happens* after you die?" and all at once she was present to me in a way she rarely was. She was no longer on stage. She was no longer in character. She had stepped off into the wings for a moment, and the words she had spoken were not in the script. Her face was for the moment not the one she had skillfully assembled in front of her dressing-table mirror that morning with lipstick, powder, and eyebrow pencil, but her own true face.

She had come a long way from the little girl in frilly white with the upside-down flowers in her lap. She was in her eighties with bad arthritis in her knees and was wearing whichever one of her many hearing aids she happened to have chosen that day, although none of them ever seemed to do her much good. I always suspected that it was not so much because she was deaf that she couldn't hear, but because there was so much she didn't want to hear that she chose to be deaf. To get anything through to her you had to say it at the top of your lungs, so in answer to her question, I said YES. I said I believed SOMETHING HAPPENS. But there are things that cannot be shouted, and as soon as I tried in my more or less normal voice to tell her a little more about what I believed and why I believed it, I could see that she was not only not hearing, but also not listening. Just to have asked the question seemed for the time being to be as much as she could handle.

So later, when I got home, I tried to answer the question in a letter. I wrote her I believe that what happens when you die is that, in ways I knew no more about than she did, you are given back your life again, and I said there were three reasons why I believed it. First, I wrote her, I believed it because, if I were God and loved the people I created and wanted them to become at last the best they had it in them to be, I couldn't imagine consigning them to oblivion when their time came with the job under the best of circumstances only a fraction done. Second, I said, I believed it, apart from any religious considerations, because I had a hunch it was true. I intuited it. I said that if the victims and the victimizers, the wise and the foolish, the good-hearted and the heartless all end up alike in the grave and that is the end of it, then life would be a black comedy, and to me, even at its worst, life doesn't *feel* like a black comedy. It feels like a *mystery*. It feels as though, at the innermost heart of it, there is Holiness, and that we experience all the horrors that go on both around us and within us *as* horrors rather than as just the way the cookie crumbles because, in our own innermost hearts, we belong to Holiness, which they are a tragic departure from. And lastly, I wrote her, I believe that what happens to us after we die is that we aren't dead forever because Jesus said so.

Jesus was another of the dead people I knew my mother wouldn't want to talk about, and I had no idea how she would react to my invoking his authority. I said that, because in one way Jesus was a human being like the rest of us, I imagined he could be wrong about lots of things like the rest of us too and probably believed the world was flat just the way everybody else did in his day. But when he said to the Good Thief on the cross next to his, "Today shalt thou be with me in Paradise," I wrote her, I would bet my bottom dollar that he of all people knew what he was talking about, because if in one way he was a human being, in another way he was immeasurably more.

I could hardly conceive of a more unlikely person than my mother to have written such a letter to, but since trying to shout it all to her instead was unthinkable, I mailed it anyway, and when I asked about it some weeks later, her only answer was to say that it had made her cry. I don't think that it was anything I said that made her cry; in fact, I doubt if she even read my letter all the way through. I think that it was being reminded by the letter of her original question about death. I think her tears had to do with what she saw as the pathos of simply having asked it when she knew without ever talking about it that her own death couldn't be all that far away.

The only time I can remember *seeing* her cry was sometime during her late fifties when she had to have most of her upper teeth pulled and, on returning from the ordeal, threw herself face down on her bed, where for an hour or more she sobbed her heart out over what she must have felt was the end of the world. If she cried when my father committed suicide in 1936, when he was thirty-eight and she was forty, I never saw her do it; nor on the rare occasions when she talked about him during the half century and more that she survived him did I ever sense that behind her words there were tears that she was holding back. The sadness of other people's lives, even the people she loved, never seemed to touch her where she lived. I don't know why. It wasn't that she had a hard heart, I think—in many ways she was warm, sympathetic, generous— but that she had a heart that for one reason or another she kept permanently closed to other people's suffering, as well as to the darkest corners of her own.

■ ■ ■

Why not bring her, like Naya, to my Magic Kingdom to ask her about it? I think that more than anything else it is because I am afraid. I am afraid of what she might say. I am afraid of what I might say. I am afraid of her.

In an earlier memoir called *Telling Secrets*, which I delivered first as a series of three lectures before an audience some thousand strong in the ballroom of a New York hotel, I told a number of secrets about her and about my complex feelings about her. Not daring to do it while she was still alive, I gave as honest a picture of her as I knew how. I described the New York apartment where she lived the last thirty years or so of her life and the room in it where just short of ninety-two she died—her dressing table laden with beauty preparations and gadgets, the patent medicines on the bureau, the chaise lounge with the fake leopard-skin throw and dozens of little pillows, the beaded Victorian pincushions, the movie magazines. I told about what I always felt was the curse upon her of having been born blue-eyed and beautiful, with the result that she never had to be especially kind and loving in order to draw people to her because they were drawn to her anyway. I told about my father and his death and a little about her marriage to him. They weren't very many or very terrible, these secrets I told about her, but they were all of them secrets that for almost a century she had kept not only from the world, but much of the time from herself, and as I stood up there at the lectern spilling them out to that huge room full of strangers, I felt sure that if she happened to turn up with a gun in her hands, she would shoot me dead without turning a hair.

I saw her for the last time a couple of months before she died. She was sitting up in bed. She had let her hair go whiter than I had ever seen it before and was wearing almost no makeup. She was looking not at me as she spoke, but down at her covers, and her words were mainly about her various aches and pains, her sleepless nights, her burning feet, the red patch that appeared on her cheek every morning and that she had to spend hours working at with face powder and cold cream to conceal. *Agony* was the word she used to describe it all, which I took to be a characteristic exaggeration. She excoriated the woman who came to stay with her nights for not giving her the bourbon and Valium she asked for to help her sleep. She excoriated my brother for his barbaric neglect. When I pointed out that the night woman was only following the doctor's orders and that she had no more devoted slave in the world than my brother, she was furious. I was totally unsympathetic as usual, she said. I never took her side in anything. "Why do you hate me?" she asked, and when I protested that if I hated her, I would not have come all the way down from Vermont to see her, she replied, simply in order to cause her pain and that I had refused to stop so she could go to the bathroom the last time I had driven back from Vermont with her. Suddenly I found myself storming out of her room so full of anger that I might never have gone back, and that would have been the dismal way our last encounter ended. Even as I was going, I saw a queer look of satisfaction on her face. She had gotten a rise out of me. She had goaded me into demonstrating the very hate I had just finished denying.

But then some good angel gave me pause. She was old. She was falling to pieces. Her world was falling to pieces. Maybe agony was closer to the truth of it than I supposed. So I went back after a few moments, and neither of us made any mention of what had just taken place. We talked for a while. Her tiny doctor appeared and bound up one arthritic knee swollen to the size of a melon. And then, as I was finally leaving, she said to me, "You have always been my hero."

"Why do you hate me?" and "You have always been my hero." Those were the last two things I can remember her ever having said to me face to face.

■ ■ ■

"Why do you tell all these intimate things?" I hear her ask now. Her tone is not accusatory this time. It is hushed, intimate.

"So I can forget them?" I say. "To put them on record so they will never be forgotten?"

"You didn't cry into your typewriter when you heard I'd died," she says.

"I cried when we buried your ashes."

My brother and my wife and I had taken them out in a cardboard box to Irwin, Pennsylvania, near Pittsburgh, where we buried them in the Long Run Cemetery next to Naya and my grandfather and other Kuhn forebears going back to the eighteenth century. Over her grave I had read the passage from Revelation that describes the holy city with its walls of sapphire, emerald, topaz, and its twelve gates of pearl because she had always loved pretty things, and then as I was saying the benediction I suddenly found myself choked by a wrenching yelp of whatever it was a yelp of—grief, regret, divine relief. Unutterable love.

"That cheap little pot of ferns you left at my grave from the supermarket across the street," she says.

"It was all they had," I say. "We laughed to think what you'd have said if you knew."

"I'll bet you did," she says.

■ ■ ■

The Magic Kingdom is magically still. Naya has left her knitting in the wing chair and is standing by the window looking out. She has one finger on the glass pane.

"You ask me to rattle on about death," she says. "That is like my asking you to rattle on about life. Where would you begin?

Where would you end? What could you compare life to when life is all you know?

"In life you *move forward*. That is what life is all about. 'Leg over leg the dog went to Dover,' as your grandfather was fond of quoting at the drop of a hat. From Pittsburgh we went leg over leg to Saranac the winter Ruth had trouble with her lungs and stayed there through spring despite the bitter recriminations of your mother, who had her heart set on graduating from Miss Mitchell's with her class so she could go marching down the aisle of Calvary Church with a bunch of long-stemmed roses in her arms. When we didn't spend the whole summer in Machiasport, we would often go to Saint-Jean-de-Luz or Thun, almost always ending up in Geneva to see Tante Elise Golay, who lived up in the old part of the city under the shadow of Calvin's grim cathedral with a cherry tree in her yard that had a bell in it which she could pull with a string to frighten the birds away. After your poor father died, I went to Bermuda with your mother and you boys to help you get settled there, and what a fairy tale of an island it was in those days, with the silvery bells of the bicycles and the narrow little railway and the horses and carriages. And if you were feeling grand and thought you could raise the price, you could ride that trolley to see those dear little pink and blue cottages with their white roofs like cupcakes. To be alive is to keep moving on and on like that, even if it's only upstairs to bed at night or down to Trade Street to get that nice young Mr. Landrum to cash your meager check for you at the bank, or maybe just to see the sights like Mrs. E. Scruggs Brown, O wondrous name, in her fur piece or old C. J. Lynch, the real estate tycoon, with his extraordinary nose, standing in a doorway tipping his straw hat to all the ladies.

"And to be alive is, of course, always to keep moving

through time too, as day follows day follows day like circus elephants holding each other's tails. You move from one time to another time to another time until finally your time runs out. That is what life is all about. But you asked me about death."

There is not much snow on the ground outside the window, but there is enough to leave it mostly white. The meadow and wooded hill beyond are lost in the November mist. Naya has one hand on her hip as she gazes out at it. There is a knitting needle stuck into her gray bun.

"Once you've stepped off the streetcar," she says, "you don't keep moving on in the same way. It's more like moving *in*— not the dog going leg over leg to Dover anymore, but instead somebody like Mr. Edison moving closer and closer to some new discovery, some revelation that will open up a whole new world, a whole new way of understanding everything. Or so you hope. I'm sorry I make it sound so uninteresting. It is really very interesting indeed."

"You make it sound lonely," I say. "Do you ever see people you used to know, people you loved?"

"My dear boy," she says. "Words like *see* don't do very well on this side of things. But yes, they are here. They are part of what, ever so slowly, we move deeper and deeper toward, or into, or through—whatever the preposition is. They are part of what we begin little by little to understand at last."

I almost don't dare to ask it, but then I do. "Is Daddy there?"

"They all are," she says.

It has been more than sixty years since that early morning in New Jersey when I saw him last, and although I remember a few isolated things about him, my father himself I can't remember. I can't remember his face or his voice. I can't remember loving him. I can't even remember remembering him.

But I do not ask Naya now to tell me whatever she can about where he is or how he is or who he is. And to bring him back now to this peaceful room full of books would be unthinkable. The reason, I think, is fear.

It is fear that keeps me from bringing my mother back, and it is fear also, I think, that keeps me from bringing my father back, although a different kind of fear. I do not bring my mother back for fear that she will be too much for me. Maybe I do not bring my father back for fear that he will be too little. Or that I will be. I suppose one way to read my whole life—my religious faith, the books I have written, the friends I have made—is as a search for him. Maybe at its heart my fear is the fear of finding him.[5]

CHAPTER 5

THE STRUGGLE OF MEMORY

Like the books in the library, the old photographs and the old letters are silent. They too are leaving me room to be myself. They are letting me be, as most of the time I try also to let them be, passing by the gray boxes as I enter the Magic Kingdom without a sideward glance. I do not want to stir them up or be stirred up by them. But even in their silence they are always present. My father has been dead for more than sixty years, but I doubt that a week has gone by without my thinking of him. In recent years I doubt that a single day has gone by. Who on earth was he? Who on earth would he have lived to become? He could even conceivably still be alive to see his hundredth birthday this summer, just as Jimmy Merrill's mother, born the same month of the same year, will see hers. Who on earth would I have become if he had lived long enough to get me through my growing up? What would he have to say to me now, or I to him?

At least I know what I would say to him as he sits there on the grass next to my mother with his face turned to look at something that nobody else seems to be noticing. Shadowed by her hat brim, my mother's gaze appears to be directed toward the photographer, but it is not the photographer she is seeing.

She is seeing beyond him to what she knows is going to happen the next day. Her eyes are filled with her secret, and her expression is very grave. Who knows all that she is seeing?

I would say to my father, "Don't do it. Get out of it any way you can, for both your sakes. You would never dream where the path you have chosen is going to lead you. Make a break for it while there's still time."

But why should he listen? There isn't a man at Lake Placid who isn't in love with the girl at his side. The rector of Trinity Church will be waiting for them the next day. The room at the Chateau Frontenac has been booked. It will all happen as planned, and among other things that will happen, I will happen. So how can I wish undone this thing they are on the threshold of doing without wishing myself undone? Even though it will cost my father his life at the age of thirty-eight, and even though it will mean my mother's taking to her grave, just short of her ninety-second birthday, a burden of guilt and regret and self-condemnation that as far as I know she never spoke about to a living soul let alone to me. I would not have missed the shot at the world that their misalliance gave me. Can I make it up to them somehow—by treasuring away their youth and beauty in the gray boxes and telling about it, by honoring them as best I can for having been father and mother to me as best they could, by forgiving them and asking their forgiveness?[6]

■ ■ ■

In the middle of this inner half of the library there is a maple drop-leaf table with both leaves extended and a chair at either side. On it there is a tall brass lamp that my daughter Dinah gave me with two slender necks arching gracefully downward like flowers, one to the left and one to the right, and ending in green glass shades. Naya has turned one of them on so that she can see the cards spread out on the table in front of her.

"At the original Canfield's, you paid fifty dollars for the pack," she says, "and they gave you five dollars back for each card you managed to play off on an ace. So far I am doing quite well, but, of course, I cheat. You're supposed to go through the pack one at a time only once, but I go through it in threes, shuffling each time, until there's not another card I can play. It seems irreverent to be gambling surrounded by all these books about God. I hope he won't mind."

There is something of Rembrandt in the way the light of the lamp has caught her face, her glasses, the table's surface, with the rest of the room in shadow.

"I don't remember that you and I ever talked much about God," I say, "but I remember that winter in Tryon when we used to go to the Episcopal church on Melrose Avenue together. It was before I went away to school."

"I'm afraid we went mainly to hear Harold Crandall in the choir," she says. "When they sang the Benedicite, he always took the solo part in his anguished, throbbing baritone—'O ye Lightnings and Clouds, bless ye the Lord. O ye whales and all that dwell in the waters, bless ye the Lord.' O ye this, that, and the other like the foghorn off Machias, and everybody else chiming in with 'Praise him and magnify him forever.' It gave us ungodly joy."

"Would you say you were a believer in those days?" I ask. She has a single card by one corner, a red queen, and is holding it hesitantly over the table looking for a place to play it.

"I was a Unitarian as much as I was anything," she says. "I believed in 'the achieving power of hopeful thought,' that lovely phrase. William Ellery Channing said it, I think. Or perhaps it was Mr. Emerson. I always believed too that there was more than met the eye."

"And how about now?" I ask.

Finding no place for the red queen, she replaces it among the cards in her hand and sets them softly down on the table.

"Well, the mystery is by no means solved, if that's what you think," she says. "On the contrary. I always felt quite at sea about it when I was on your side of things and never dwelt on it especially because there was so much else that seemed more pressing. I always assumed that when you died, you would no longer see through a glass darkly but face to face, as St. Paul quite inaccurately predicted. However, such was not the case. On the contrary, it was like stepping out of a dark house into the greater dark of night."

She pauses for a moment, glancing up into the shadows as though they are the sky. One lens of her glasses catches the lamp's light.

"The moon," she says. "The Milky Way unwinding like a scarf, the constellations. All those fathoms upon fathoms of darkness. Who knows what other moons and stars there are farther still. What deeper depths.

"You'd think it would quite take your breath away, if you had breath to take," she says. "But it doesn't, *mirabile dictu*. It's almost as if it *is* your breath." She glances down at the pattern of cards on the table for a moment. "Or as if it's breathing you."

She gathers the lot of them into a single pile then and starts arranging them so that they all face the same way. Making them into a pack, she taps it lightly on the table to square it.

There is only one window in this end of the library, and it is behind Naya's chair. Through it I can see a patch of lawn and an apple tree, beyond that the horse pasture sloping gradually up to the top of the hill where the house stands that we lived in for some thirty years before moving down to the one that belonged to my wife's parents. Until we took it over, the house on the hill was the guest house, and now it is the guest house again, the place where our daughters stay when they come with their husbands and children. On the windowsill there are several objects—a black wrought-iron bank in the shape of a dachshund, a shoeshine parlor's brass footstand as delicately curved as a Brancusi, a jester's wand with a puffy face in the middle of a five-pointed silver star hung with lavender ribbons and one tiny remaining bell that tinkles if you shake it. On top of the lower sash is a wide band of plaited straw that came from Mexico, I think. It is the Last Supper with the flattened heads of the disciples, six on one side and six on the other, and another head in the middle that you know is Jesus because of the straw cross behind it.

"Tell me about Jesus," I say.

Behind her, through the window, I can see a chestnut mare at the pasture fence. She is nibbling at the grass with a white blaze on her nose. Every now and then she sweeps her satiny flanks with her tail. The lower part of her hind legs is obscured by the plaited straw.

"There was a poem about him I loved," she says. "I can't quite bring it back, but I can hear the music of it as clearly as your voice. *Da da dum, da da dum,*" with one finger she taps it out lightly on the edge of the table.

> "You will know him when he comes
> Not by the roll of drums
> Or the clarion trumpet's blare . . .

"That's not it, but short, solemn lines like that, not unlike drumbeats themselves. The idea is you will know him when he comes not by any outward show but—oh, dear—by his something kingly tread, in some quiet inner way. Maybe it will come back to me. As a Unitarian I didn't believe in his divinity, whatever exactly that means—being of one substance with the Father and all that—but I believed what the poem says. I believed I would know him if ever I saw him, even if he was just walking down Trade Street in the rain or standing behind the counter at Ballenger's. And I believe it still."

"You haven't seen him then?"

The little straw heads on the windowsill are faceless. They are sitting with their folded arms on the table, the one in the middle leaning ever so slightly to his right. The silvery light from the window shines through the straw.

"I will know him if I do," she says. And before I know that I am going to do it, I say, "He will know you."

"Who can tell?" she says. "Sometimes when you're going someplace, you send a scrap of your heart ahead. Isn't that what you taped on the back of your little heart-shaped stone? Maybe that scrap of mine is what he will know me by. 'There are more things in heaven and earth, Horatio.' Maybe I will know him because he sent me a scrap of his."[7]

■ ■ ■

Along with his bold signature, Trollope has written "Very faithfully" on a little card beneath the photograph of him that hangs in the library, and so faithful were the likenesses he drew that I need him now to help me draw one of my brother, Jamie, who died as I was writing these last few pages. He was two and a half years younger than I am and would have been seventy on his next birthday. We were the only two children in our family. I can't imagine the world without him. I can't imagine him without the world.

I want to get him right the way Trollope would have gotten him right. I want especially to get his way of laughing right. I want to get it right about how on his visits to see us in Vermont when everybody else was dithering around trying to decide what to do next, he would sit out on the lawn in his sweater and khaki pants reading the *Times* in utter peace as he puffed on one of the appalling little cigars he wasn't allowed to smoke inside. I want to get it right about the way he took life as it came instead of, like me, brooding about the past or worrying himself sick about the future.

I also want to get it right about whatever it is that is going on inside me now. There is the level of feeling where, after moments when the clouds seem to be lifting a little, it is suddenly all I can do to see the hand in front of my face. And there is the level of thinking, thinking back especially over our last few conversations, including the one within only three or four hours of his death when we said good-bye for good. But deeper down still there is a level that I know nothing about at all except that whatever I am doing there, it is absolutely exhausting. It is as if great quantities of furniture have to be moved from one place to another. There seem to be endless cartons of God only knows what to sort through somehow. The earth itself has to be bulldozed and shifted around and reshaped. A whole new landscape has to come into being.

As legend has it, I was taken to see him for the first time at Miss Lippincott's, a New York lying-in hospital where it was fashionable to be born at this period, when he was only a day or so old. According to my mother, he was a scrawny little thing, and to make up for it she was eager for the nurses and doctors to see her cherubic firstborn as well. My father was the one who brought me, and, according again to my mother, I put on a horrifying act as he led me to her room, walking all doubled over with my eyes rolling around in my head and my jaw hanging loose. But apparently things looked up as soon as I saw the baby. I said I wanted to recite him something, and I did. What I chose was, "One misty moisty morning when cloudy was the weather, I chanced to meet an old man all dressed up in leather," and it marked the beginning of a relationship that lasted for just short of seventy years.

For the first seven or eight of them, I'm afraid that in the way of big brothers I made his life miserable. At that point the two and a half years' difference in our ages seemed to put us in different generations, and I must have felt that it was bad enough simply to have a rival at all, let alone one whose youth and lack of experience were a continual source of embarrassment to me. When we lived in Washington, D.C., in 1932 I was sent off to first grade at a school run by two French spinsters known as the Misses Maret, where all classes were conducted in the French language, including music, which we were taught by an old lady who played the piano in spite of being blind as a bat so that we spent most of the time making terrible faces at her with no fear of reprisal. Apparently I let my brother walk part of the way to school with me, but always made him turn back well before we got there so nobody would discover my shame.

I have that detail only on my mother's word, but I actually remember one summer in Quogue, Long Island, sticking a wad of bubble gum in his hair so that when Energine failed to get rid of it, it had to be cut out with scissors, leaving a disfiguring patch of bald scalp, and on another occasion throwing a fat green caterpillar at him, which sent him into hysterics when it burst to pieces on his shirt. Sometimes I would simply look at him and gibber nonsense syllables until he could take it no longer and started to scream. For fear the racket would bring our parents' wrath down upon me, I developed a sure-fire technique for stopping him. If only he would be quiet, I said, I would give him my Uncle Wiggily books, and it always worked like a charm. Most of them have my name in them, Frebby, but you can see where in one or two he managed to add his too, using an electrically heated stylus we had that you could write with through strips of variously colored gold, silver, and bronze metallic paper. Probably because he knew the transaction would never hold up in court, he always seemed to take it for granted that in time the books reverted automatically to me, and thus the bribe worked for years. I also told him that he was a foundling someone had left on our doorstep in a basket and that when he walked, his corduroy knickerbockers squeaked in a ridiculous way and that his garters showed. This was roughly at the time when, at the arrival of some visitors in our house, we could hear him muttering something over and over again under his breath, and when we asked him later what it had been, he said it was the number six, six, six, six, because he knew they would probably ask him how old he was and he wanted to be ready with the answer. Every once in a while when we were in our fifties or so he would suddenly turn on me and cry out, "You ruined my childhood!" to which I would answer that he was ruining my old age, and then, together, we would rock with seismic laughter.

I suppose it was by a gradual process that we changed from victim and victimizer to best friends, but a major step along the way must have come soon after dawn on Saturday, November 21, 1936, when Jamie was a month short of eight and I only a few months past ten. Staying in our room as we had been told, we looked down from what seemed a dizzying height to where our mother and grandmother in their nightdresses had managed to drag the young man who was our father from the garage out onto the driveway and, with no idea in the world how to do it, were trying to revive him. I picture us up there as we would have appeared from below. We are framed by the window in our pajamas, and in different ways for each of us I suspect that we remained there, side by side, always.[8]

■ ■ ■

As nearly as it is possible to reenter myself in those days, it seems to me that I had somehow managed to put that shadow so far behind me or deep within me that it was as if it had never been at all. We lived surrounded by fields of Easter lilies and Bermuda onions, by white coral roads that dried in minutes after even the most torrential rain, by pink coral beaches that we biked to after school to swim in Gulf Stream waters that went from aquamarine to turquoise to celery green as they neared the shore. The air was fragrant with the dwarf cedars that grew everywhere in those days, before they were killed by the blight, and the complex scent of horses, kerosene stoves, and the salt sea air. In the midst of all that, for me, everything that had come earlier vanished without a trace. But not so for Jamie.

I came upon him once all by himself in his bedroom crying, and when I asked him why, he wouldn't tell me. Was it this? Was it that? But all he would finally say was that it was something that had happened a long time ago—a year is a long time when you've lived so few of them—and only then did I realize with a jolt that he was of course crying about our father. I would never have known of it except by accident, he would never have told me if I hadn't dragged it out of him, and all his life he remained such a profoundly private person that when I wrote a fictionalized version of our childhood called *The Wizard's Tide*, for his sake I changed him into a little girl. He kept his feelings almost entirely to himself, didn't like "direct questions" as he put it, and I remember my delight in overhearing the way he handled one once at a cocktail party in Florida. A very energetic, cause-oriented woman asked him what he did with his life now that he had retired, and what he said to her was that the first thing he did every morning was count the sections of his breakfast grapefruit and that she might be interested to know the number was by no means always the same.

Needless to say, the feelings remained deep down inside him, although not because he had unconsciously repressed them there, I think, but simply because deep down was where, like a furnace in the cellar, he felt they belonged. Only on the rarest occasions did they ever surface. Once when he was leafing through *Listening to Your Life*, a collection of quotations from my books for every day of the year, I asked him to look up and read me the one for his birthday, December 7. It turned out to be a passage about how when our mother was in her nineties, she asked me one day who the man was that had just passed by her window and, when I told her it was the gardener, said, "Tell him to come in and take a look at the last rose of summer." Suddenly, he stopped in the middle of a sentence and I could see that he could read no further. Another time was when he went with us once to what turned out to be an extraordinarily moving Blanche Moyse performance of the *St. Matthew Passion* in Marlboro, Vermont, and after it was over, when I asked him what he had thought of it, he was literally unable to speak.

He wrote a poem or two in the guest book we tried to keep for a while. "Japanese candy tastes like punk. / That's the word for today from Uncle Skunk" one of them goes, and another, perhaps even more eloquent, "I tied a daisy to a rock. / When I threw it into Beebe Pond, it went plock."

He also collected malapropisms he enjoyed using from time to time like "eyebulb," "red leather day," and "you might as well be hung for a sheep as a goat," and when he retired from the bank where for years he worked without much enthusiasm as a public relations officer, he took to puttering around with electronics in their apartment in a nineteenth-century Madison Avenue brownstone, where he and his wife, Jackie, lived for all the years of their marriage. It was my mother who rented it first in 1946, so the way Jamie reckoned it, it has been in the family for something like half of its existence. When my mother married for the third time and moved out of it down to North Carolina, I lived there alone for a time, trying to write one early novel or another. Sunday after Sunday I would go to the church next door to hear George Buttrick preach sermons that ended up changing my life and eventually started off from there to attend Union Theological Seminary for the first time, making the trip on the Number Four Fifth Avenue bus, which went up as far as the Cloisters and Fort Tryon Park as, for all I know, it still does. In 1954 when Jamie got out of the army, where he ended up as a second lieutenant at Fort Sill, Oklahoma, he and I lived there together for a time. It was during this period that we drove south to visit our mother, who decided to use our presence as an excuse for throwing a large cocktail party "to meet James and Frederick Buechner" as the invitation read, which made it sound, we decided, as though she was announcing our engagement.

The apartment that, with his wife, Jamie lived in all those years and finally died in is on the third floor, up a flight of fifty-two sagging, dimly lit steps, and in a small room off the living room he worked at a table turning out strange flickering, beeping electronic devices that he housed in the little wooden boxes that dried codfish comes in. Two of the ones he made for me still work. One of them is a cross that blinks, first the horizontal beam marked OPEN, and then the vertical one marked HEART, which comes down through the E with a small red heart at the end of OPEN to balance things out the way I described it in the second of the Bebb books; and the other is a delicate, matchstick rendition of the Emerald City with three turrets, each bearing a green pennant marked OZ, that at the push of a button tinkles out a tiny, electronic version of "Over the Rainbow." He made a good many of them over the years for various friends and relations, several of them boxes that would answer any question you put to them with YES, NO, or MAYBE. When he was trying to decide what to call them, I suggested *ignis fatuus*, which he liked though neither of us ever got around to figuring out what the plural would be.

Our father's death never seemed to haunt him the way, for more than sixty years, it has haunted me, partly, I think, because he laid it to rest by grieving over it, whereas both my mother and I carried on as though the man had never even lived, let alone died. Partly, too, I think it was because he was just enough younger than I not to have been so affected by all the sadness and disorder that surrounded it, although there was one period, during which we were staying at Naya's house on Woodland Road while our father was off looking for yet another job, when under the pretext that his clothes didn't fit right he refused more or less for an entire winter to get up and dressed in the mornings because, I can only guess, bed was the safest, sanest, most comforting place he knew. But mainly, I suspect, it was simply not in his nature to dwell on the past any more than it was to agonize about the future. Even during the last year of his life this was so. He was subjected to all sorts of painful medical and surgical procedures that I would have ruined weeks of my life dreading, whereas he took them as completely in his stride as trips to the dentist. When he finally learned that there was nothing more the doctors could do for him except try to control the increasing pain, I disregarded his distaste for direct questions and asked him how he felt about it. His answer was simply that he looked forward to its all being over soon more than he had ever looked forward to anything in his life.

The last time we met was a month or so before the fatal diagnosis was made. I had to speak at Trinity Church on Wall Street and made a detour on my way from Penn Station to see him. It was a brief, hectic visit, most of which I spent trying to find out with the help of a map he produced where on earth in the bowels of Manhattan my hotel was and how I was going to get there. He had lost a fair amount of weight by then and a good deal of energy, but he looked well, his color was good, and he seemed to have no doubt that everything was going to be all right. Though the fifty-two steps were something of a challenge, he said, he made himself go out every day, and when it came time for me to leave, he said he would leave with me. It was a sunny, windy spring day on Madison Avenue, and we spoke about how he and Jackie would be coming up for my birthday in a few weeks. Then a taxi appeared so suddenly that

I barely had time to shake his hand before I was off on my way, not dreaming that we would never shake hands again.

What did he look like? Trollope sometimes tells you so much—describing in turn the hair, brow, eyes, lips, teeth, nose—that you end up seeing everything except the face they all add up to. He was on the short side, well built, a little thick around the middle in his later years but with his wife's constant vigilance always managing to trim down before it got out of hand. When he was young, people thought he looked like the young Bobby Kennedy. When he was older, he told our mother one day that when he was standing in front of the bathroom mirror before he had shaved his stubble that morning, he decided he was a dead ringer for Yasir Arafat, to which her reply was that he should be so lucky. Maybe what people remember most vividly about him is his laugh—not just the way he did it, with his head thrown back, putting all he had into it, all he *was* into it, holding back nothing—but the way you could see him getting ready to do it, waiting for you to set it off by doing something or saying something funnier than anything you could possibly have managed without him. My laughter when it gets out of control becomes a series of falsetto hoots that embarrass me because they don't sound at all like who I think I am, but his was totally who he was, the richest and the best of himself that he had to give. We had only to think of something along the lines of his theatrical debut as Alice with long golden curls in a Trinity School production of the Mad Tea Party—Jamie was in the third grade, I was in the sixth, and a little oddball named Truman Capote was in the seventh— and we would fall to pieces. Or to remember something like our mother's remark, apropos of his ultraconservative taste in clothes, that whenever she went looking for a necktie to give

THE MAGIC OF MEMORY

him for his birthday, she always told the clerk that she was
buying it for her grandfather.

He had hazel eyes and strong, white teeth, and his feet
sometimes tended to turn out a little when he walked. He
had a good head of hair and never wore hats except a knitted
wool one pulled down to his eyebrows when he came up to
see us winters. When we went walking in the snow, he often
carried an ash staff about as tall as he was, which one or the
other of our daughters had cut and decorated for him. Into the
bark she carved a heart, a cross like the one on the Swiss flag
surrounded by a shield, and his initials, J. K. B. Underneath,
spiraling downwards, is the word *salzstengel*, which for reasons
long forgotten was some kind of a family joke, and beneath it
Mum Mum, which was what he was apt to say when he was
about to dig into, or "fang" as he sometimes put it, some dish
that he was especially fond of. At the bottom it says Christmas
1978. It leans now against the back wall of the guest-room
closet where he last left it.

He was an unassuming man—he assumed nothing about
the people he met, plain or fancy, except that the chances were
he would find something about them that was either interesting or entertaining. And an unpretentious man—he made
no pretense at being anything he wasn't but seemed to accept
himself for better or worse the way he accepted pretty much
everybody else. For years he was a shy, rather quiet man until
you got to know him, but over the years his gregarious, sup-
portive wife, whom he loved, brought him out a good deal. For
reasons known only to them, they never had any children, but
if it bothered him, he never said so. As far as I know, he never
bore a grudge, and I can't remember ever hearing him speak
a cruel word or a deceitful one. I have never known anybody

braver. As an old friend wrote in a sentence that sounds a little like the great Anthony himself, "He was always for me one of the loveliest men I had ever come to know."

It was on July 11, 1998, the day I turned seventy-two, that he phoned me to say that he had been told he had incurable cancer of virtually everything and didn't intend to be around for more than two weeks more if he could possibly help it. He then added, "By the way, Happy Birthday," at which he managed somehow to give his extraordinary laugh once again, with some fractured, hopeless echo of it from me. "I've told Jackie to think of it not as losing a husband but as gaining half a closet." I told him that I would come down right away to New York to see him, but though he never in so many words asked me not to—there wasn't much to see was what he said—I knew that was the way he wanted it. And it was the way I wanted it too. The alternative, we came to agree, was too harrowing to think about. Instead, we talked almost every day on the telephone, and that way we could go on believing that there would always be another time still and another time after that, whereas a last visit would be the last and we both would know it.

When I called him on the afternoon of Saturday, July 25, I said, remembering about his two-week deadline, that it must be that the end wasn't very far off. He said that it had already started and that it was the happiest day of his life. Although he was a dying man, he in no way either sounded or seemed like a sick man. He said how good it had been to see Judy earlier in the day. She had gone down to be with Jackie, and I decided I had to go with her despite the earlier agreement, but was saved by a cold and fever. I told him that I had loved him as much as I had ever loved anybody in my life, and forgetting about the green caterpillar and the bubble gum, he said, "You have been a wonderful brother." I said I had a feeling we had not seen the last of each other, and he made a soft, descending "Ah-h-h" sound as a way to thank me for saying it, for maybe even believing it. Then I said I guessed this was good-bye, and he said yes, and then we both started to cry so that there was nothing more we could do but hang up, he in the old brownstone on Madison Avenue and I in what our grandson, Dylan, calls "the breakable room," rarely used because it is filled with things too precious to risk breaking and now with this other precious thing.

One of our sons-in-law, David, was with him when he died a few hours later, and Jamie told him how he wished he knew how to thank him properly for all he had done, flying down from Boston four or five times those last few days to help him wind things up in every conceivable way. He said he wished he had some way to repay him for his inconceivable kindness, to which David replied that I had once said I might think about giving him the Uncle Wiggily books. "If I were you, I'd try to get that in writing," Jamie said, and those were among the last of all his words.

He never went to church except once in a while to hear me, and he didn't want a funeral, he told me—too much like a direct question, I suppose—but when I suggested maybe cocktails and dinner for some of his old friends in the fall when everybody got back to the city, he said that sounded like a good idea. But he did ask me if I would write a prayer for him that he could use, and David said that he had it there on the table beside him.

"Dear Lord, bring me through darkness into light. Bring me through pain into peace. Bring me through death into life. Be with me wherever I go, and with everyone I love. In Christ's name I ask it. Amen."[9]

■ ■ ■

St. Paul, or whoever it was, wrote to the Ephesians that he always remembered them in his prayers, asking God, among other things, to give them "a spirit of revelation in the knowledge of him," which is just about what you would expect him to ask. But then he added an explanatory phrase that I, for one, would not have expected and maybe for that reason never even noticed until it jumped off the page at me the other day— "having the eyes of your heart enlightened, that you may know what is the hope to which he has called you." *The eyes of your heart*, of course, is the phrase. "O altitudo!" as Sir Thomas Browne would have said—to find such words where I never found them before and just when I needed them. That day on the staircase when I met my first grandchild for the first time, what I saw with the eyes of my head was a very small boy with silvery gold hair and eyes the color of blue denim coming down toward me in his mother's arms. What I saw with the eyes of my heart was a life that without a moment's hesitation I would have given my life for. To look through those eyes is to see every kingdom as magic.

"The hope to which he has called you" is what you will see with them, says Ephesians, and suddenly in this quiet, book-filled room where I sit with my feet up and a cup of tepid coffee at my elbow, everything I see with them speaks of that hope. On one of the shelves of American fiction there is a glass ball that snows inside when you shake it, the white flakes tumbling slowly down on Dorothy, who has been overcome by the deadly poppy field with Toto at her side and the faithful Tin Woodman standing beside her with one hand raised to his brow as he peers out for something to deliver her. With the eyes of his tin head he does not see that it is the snow itself that will do it by waking her up, as the movie has it. Or that it is he and the Scarecrow who will end up carrying her to safety, according to the book. Or that one way or another it is, of course, no less than L. Frank Baum, the wizard himself, who will see to it that in the long run nothing, not even the Wicked Witch and her legions, will be able to destroy these creatures whom he loves, because they are his and because it is in him that they live and move and have their being. He cannot see all this with the eyes of his heart because, of course, the wizard has not yet given him a heart.

Ganesh is nearby on the same shelf—Ganesh the debonair and gentle, Parvati's son and gate-keeper, whose head Siva lopped off in a fit of pique only to feel sorry afterward and replace it with the head of an elephant. He is made of terracotta and sits pot-bellied and four-armed with his toys in his hands—an elephant goad, a string of beads, a bowl for alms, something that looks like a television remote control. His trunk is curled artfully just above his left breast, and his right leg is tucked under him. He has a kind of triple tiara on his head reminiscent of the one the pope wears on gala occasions. When he rides, he rides on a rat, which is small and cunning enough to thread its way through anything, and when he walks, he tramples all obstacles underfoot or uproots them with his trunk. He is the bestower of prosperity and well-being, and it is said that nothing should be begun, not even the worship of another god, without first honoring him. I honor him by asking his help in hoping for what I have seen with my heart.

I hope that it is true about God. I hope that it is true about Jesus. I hope that maybe it is true even that Jamie and I haven't seen the last of each other. He said "Ah-h-h" when I said it to him, the "Ah-h-h" you comfort a child with, or of being comforted by a child as I was not long ago by my grandson Dylan. We were in the hammock together, and when we finished reading *Ant and Bee and the Rainbow* for something like the hundred and fiftieth time, we lay there for a while just looking up through the trembling leaves to the topmost branches of the maples some sixty feet above our heads and decided that you would have to be a bird to get up there. Or an angel, Dylan said—he was four at the time—which turned our conversation in another direction. Someday he would be an angel himself, he said, and I said that would not be for a very, very long time. I would get to be an angel long before he did if I got to be one at all, I told him, but I would wait for him, and then he said, "When I get there I will follow you wherever you go."

"Ah-h-h," I said.[10]

CHAPTER 6

THE HOPE
OF MEMORY

D o you really believe anything *happens* after you die?" my
mother asked me once in a suddenly hushed, intimate
voice as if to reassure me that whatever I said would go no
further. So when I got home, I wrote her the answer I couldn't
shout and I suspect she never read. But now she knows the
answer in a way that I cannot, who knows only the hope that
I see with the eyes of my heart. Is that hope anything more
than an *ignis fatuus*? Either my mother knows that too or else
she knows nothing at all because there is nothing of her left
except what's in the cardboard box that I asked Jamie to be the
one to place in the small, square hole in Irwin, Pennsylvania,
thinking about how for so long he had been the one to do
everything else she needed done. Does anything really *happen*
after you die? How would she answer that now if Jimmy were
still around to get hold of her on his Ouija board?

I know what my father would say because once he said it.
At least maybe it was my father. I haven't played with a Ouija
board for years because, Jimmy's experience notwithstanding,
I have always found something dim and slightly unwholesome
about it, but once a few years ago I tried writing out a dialogue
between my father and me using my left hand, because the

THE MAGIC OF MEMORY

childish scrawl it produced seemed to put me in touch with the child I was when I knew him and—who can say?—maybe with him too. "I've been so worried. I've been so scared," my left hand wrote, and then he wrote back, "Don't be. There's nothing to worry about. That's the secret I never knew, but I know it now." I have the manuscript still, and it is so clumsily written that I can hardly make it out. "What do you know, Daddy?" it reads, and then his answer: "I know plenty, and it's all good."

If only Ganesh could clear the way for me with his great trunk, lend me his rat to find a path through the maze. Can it be true what I've seen with my heart's eyes? Can it be that what my father said is true, that in some sense it was truly my father who said it? Can it be true that Jamie and I have not seen the last of each other? His widow writes that she is haunted by the image of "his sweet head bowed in final release," and now I am haunted by it. I cannot bring myself to think of that image as the end of everything he was.

"Well, I can tell you that at least you haven't seen the last of me," Naya says, and it is true that I do all but see her. She is wearing a white linen dress that I remember from Tryon days, when she would sit out on the terrace in a wicker peacock chair with the Blue Ridge Mountains in the distance behind her. She is sitting now in a chair catty-cornered to mine in the library. On her right is the large triple window with Jimmy's head on the sill and various objects scattered around including the heart-shaped stone from Outer Fame. On her left is the fireplace with the tray John Kouwenhoven made me out of cigarette-box wrappers on the mantel.

"In answer to your mother's question, *I* have happened anyhow," she says.

Or is it only a vision of her that has happened, of how she

looked all those years ago when everybody was alive still? Is it only a dream that I have conjured up, choosing words with great care to evoke her as best I can? I try to conjure up Jamie. Just for a moment he stands in the shadowy, inner part of the library at the opposite end from the large window, the part where the biographies are and the table with the double-headed brass lamp. He looks ruddy and fit in his khakis and a blue Brooks Brothers shirt with the sleeves rolled up. His head is tipped slightly back as if he is getting ready to laugh at something he seems to think I am getting ready to say.

"Why say *only* a vision, my poor ignorant child," she says, "*only* a dream—you of all people, with your religious turn of mind? Unlike you, I was never a great admirer of St. Paul. He always struck me as pig-headed and irascible in addition to being given to sentences so long and tangled that half the time I don't think even he was quite sure what he was getting at. But every once in a while, of course, he spoke with the tongue of angels—'What no eye has seen, nor ear heard, nor the heart of man conceived, what God has prepared for those who love him, God has revealed to us through'—well, through what if not through just such visions and dreams as you brush aside with your 'only'?"

I say, "I'm not just putting all those words in your mouth?" and she says, "No more, you might say, than I am putting them in yours."

The skirt of her white dress is dazzling with the sun on it, the upper part of it in shadow. How can I describe her face? It is mottled like the pages of an old book. Her hair is gray and parted just off center. When I was a child, Jamie and I used to watch how she would hold the comb first to her nose and then draw it slowly up her forehead till she found where the center was. Her eyes glisten under the folds of their lids, and she seems to be smiling at something that hasn't quite happened yet.

"What *has* he prepared for those who love him, then? I need to have you tell me," I say. "You know Jamie has died."

She turns her head slightly to look out the window. It is a bright, early fall morning. The leaves are still almost all of them green, but here and there you can see a spray of russet. Her sapphire ring glitters in the sun as she reaches out to touch the glass pane lightly with one finger.

"I used to knit black wool socks for him and get old Willy Westfield with the wen on the back of his neck to mail them off at the post office on his way home," she says. "He always told me they were the only ones he had that never wore out. He claimed his toenails made holes in all the others. I don't suppose he spent much time trimming them."

On the window sill there is a photograph of the two of us in a Plexiglas frame. We are standing on the beach in Florida in our bathing trunks. Jamie has a purple-and-white-striped towel around his shoulders, and I am wearing some sort of white homespun shirt. My eyes are closed, and Jamie is looking at me. We are both of us laughing.

"I always thought that when you died, all things were made plain to you," she says. "I imagined that all at once you found yourself in the heavenly presence, and everything that had ever puzzled you was a puzzle no longer, and every doubt you ever had melted into thin air the way the Apocalypse says that every tear will be wiped from our eyes, and there will be neither sorrow, nor crying, nor pain anymore—those old words that are so lovely I could almost believe they were true as I used to sit there in Calvary Church hearing them read at some poor soul's funeral."

She turns from the window and faces me again. With her elbows on the arms of the chair, she has the fingertips of her two hands touching and is looking at me over them.

"What has he prepared for those who love him?" she says, repeating my question. "Things aren't the way I always believed they were. The mystery is not only a mystery still but deeper and grander than I ever supposed. It reminds me of how, when you're looking up at the sky, sometimes there's a break in the clouds and all of a sudden, lo and behold, you catch a glimpse through it of the real sky. The most I can tell you is that I think that it's we ourselves that he's preparing. Not just the ones who love him—how like that old sinner to leave out the opposition—but the ones who don't care a fig about him one way or the other."

"Then you don't see any more, wherever you are, than I do, wherever I am?" I ask. "No lamb on his throne? Everything is still through a glass darkly?"

"I have a better seat now," she says, and for a few moments the room is still. A cloud has passed over the sun, and the hills have gone a smoky blue. "I can just picture Jimmy bent over his Ouija board with his glasses sliding down his nose, concentrating the way he used to at the tinny little piano we had in that log cabin we rented one winter. It's not that I see more than you do, but that, from where I am now, I see farther, and the farther I see, the more I come to understand how much more there is to see beyond that. And your father was right, by the by, or was it your left hand? What you see can be a little frightening sometimes, and always more than a little overwhelming, but it's as good as he said it was. I would bet my bottom dollar on that." She draws her hands apart and holds them before her in the air for a moment or two before bringing them together again with a soft, decisive little clap. "It is as good as the sky is endless," she says. "It's as good as the sky is blue, and as fair."

"Landscapes of air," I say. "It sounds so empty."

"They are all here," she says. "They are here more than you are here now with me because they are more themselves now. They are more themselves than they ever were before. And when they are together, it is the way you and that little boy were together in the hammock the other day when you were looking up into the leaves with him and you suddenly felt very *emotione*, less because of what he said than because of what as a child he was still able to be, what he helped you be for a moment with him."

"And Jamie?" I ask.

"Little by little Jamie will find himself, and little by little he will find all of us," she says. "And of course he will be found. No one is ever lost. Nothing is lost."

"Thank you," I say.

"My dear boy, you are more than welcome. I wish I'd been able to do better by you," she says. "I am a dream, but I am not only a dream. Will you remember that?"

I tell her I will remember that, and maybe I even will.

■ ■ ■

Is what she said anything like the truth? I don't mean a truth that I thought up on my own and then put into her mouth, but a truth, instead, that came to me out of God only knows where, the way Godric came to me once, and Leo Bebb, the way all my life moments have occasionally come to me when I said more than I knew and did better than I am. Who can tell?

Naya's answer to my mother's hushed, half-embarrassed question is that what happens after we die is that leg over leg, like that dog my grandfather was so fond of citing, we are off to Dover again. Dover is what God has prepared for us, she says, all of us, whether we love him or not—a Dover that, on this earthbound stretch of the road at least, no eye has seen, nor ear heard, nor heart conceived, and where we find our true selves at last and also the truth of each other and of the mystery at last. Has she any idea, I wonder, how much she sounds like her possibly least favorite saint? "Until we all attain to full maturity" is the way he puts it, and then those resounding anapests that I can't help believing she must have admired in spite of herself, "to the measure of the stature of the fullness of Christ," followed so quietly then by "speaking the truth in love, we are to grow up in every way into him."

Well, Amen and Amen is all I can say. Let it be true because I want it to be true. I feel in my bones that it is true. Sometimes I feel that it is beginning to be true, at least a little, even in me. As I grow older, less inhibited, dottier, I find it increasingly easy to move toward being who I truly am, let the chips fall where they may. I also find it easier to relate to others as they truly are too, which is at its heart, I suspect, rather a good deal like the rest of the human race including me. I find myself addressing people I hardly know as though I have known them always and taking the risk of saying things to them that, before I turned seventy, I wouldn't have dreamed of saying. Not long ago a young woman was here from Switzerland with Dinah and her family, and because she seemed unhappy with herself somehow and unaware of how beautiful she was, I *told* her how beautiful she was. And at a church coffee hour of all things, after playing ticklemouse with my grandson Tristan for a while to keep him occupied till his mother was ready to go home, I told an unknown woman standing nearby that there was a ticklemouse on the loose so she had better watch her step, at which she gave every evidence, I thought, of being rather more pleased than otherwise by the prospect of possibly running into it herself. Years ago when I first started giving lectures and readings here and there, I rather dreaded the question-and-answer sessions that usually followed them, nervous that I wouldn't know what or how to respond and that the audience would see me for the impostor I more than half suspected I was. Now, on the other hand, it is the part of such junkets that I look forward to most, and I find myself responding to people I have never set eyes on before as though they are members of my own family.

The risk, of course, is that I will make a fool of myself, or worse, as I did at a jam-packed, deafening party not long ago when I heard myself telling the hostess that it was an insult to be asked to such a thing, because it had nothing whatever to do with real conviviality but was just a misguided way of paying off social debts, which everybody there would have jumped at the chance of writing off for the sake of being allowed to stay home. But it has been my experience that the risks are far outweighed by the rewards, chief of which is that when you speak to strangers as though they are friends, more often than not, if only for as long as the encounter lasts, they become friends, and if in the process they also think of you as a little peculiar, who cares? In fact it seems to me that I often feel freer to be myself in the company of stranger-friends than in the company of those with whom there is such a long tradition of reserve and circumspection that it is hard to transcend it. I feel closer to a man I know only as Rich and see only when I go to the post office where he works, and more nourished by the banter that passes between us, than is the case with many another whom I've known for years.

"Don't imagine, son, that these are things people need to know," are the words Jimmy imagined his mother saying in response to his sexual revelations, but it is in Jimmy's voice that

I hear them now spoken to me, the same languidly modulated tone that he used when he referred to the first of my Noble lectures at Harvard, which he attended, as my "mad scene" and when, on being told that a certain poet and his wife were back in town as full of beans as ever, he said without skipping a beat, "Has-beans." These senescent *betises* of yours, I can hear him saying in the same voice. Wouldn't I do better not to bring them up at all as well as to exert myself never to make one again? That way I might be able to escape being reduced prematurely to a "character," a slippered pantaloon in holy orders—a *Presbyterian* pantaloon, he says. What he is thinking of, I suspect, are the far wilder risks he took with his own life by never in the slightest degree trying to seem like other people, not even as a child at Lawrenceville when the pressure to do so could be so brutal, but always remaining the Different Person, the Ugly, he knew himself to be, and by continuing to live as a practicing homosexual ("Practice makes perfect" I hear him say in that voice again) even after he knew the consequences could be fatal.

I think, by contrast, of how timorous I have been not only in my life but in these now four volumes of memoirs that I have written, in which I have touched from time to time on the dark guest who dwells in us all but have never risked laying fully bare the lust, the anger, the childishness, the paralyzing anxiety that are so helplessly part of who I am. "Only the young die good," the former dean of a great English cathedral wrote me at the time of Princess Diana's death. "We live by myths and fairy tales. What if Romeo in middle age becomes lecherous and corpulent and Juliet irritable and prone to migraines? I look in my mirror and see this raddled old cynic, duplicitous, hypocritical, and selfish. And once I was a beautiful young priest. I could have been so remembered if I had died at thirty-nine."

I have never risked much in disclosing the little I have of the worst that I see in my mirror, and I have not been much more daring in disclosing the best. I have seen with the eyes of my heart the great hope to which he has called us, but out of some shyness or diffidence I rarely speak of it, and in my books I have tended to write about it for the most part only obliquely, hesitantly, ambiguously, for fear of losing the ear and straining the credulity of the readers to whom such hope seems just wishful thinking. For fear of overstating, I have tended especially in my nonfiction books to understate, because that seemed a more strategic way of reaching the people I would most like to reach who are the ones who more or less don't give religion the time of day. But maybe beneath that lies the fear that if I say too much about how again and again over the years I have experienced holiness—even here I find myself drawing back from saying God or Jesus—as a living, healing, saving presence in my life, then I risk being written off as some sort of embarrassment by most of the people I know and like.

For the most part it is only in my novels that I have allowed myself to speak unreservedly of what with the eyes of my heart I have seen. When old Godric makes out the face of Christ in the leaves of a tree and realizes that the lips are soundlessly speaking his name; when Antonio Parr has his vision of Christ as the Lone Ranger thundering on Silver across the lonely sage and then covers himself by adding that it may be only "a silvery trick of the failing light"; when Brendan as a scrawny, hollow-chested wreck of a boy sees angels spread out against the sky like a great wreath and hears their singing as the mercy of God; when every once in a while on even the warmest, most breathless days Kenzie Maxwell feels a stirring of chill air about his nostrils or sees a snow-white bird circling around and around in the air over him as he takes his pre-breakfast walk on the golf course—they are all of them telling my story.

To that extent I have dared risk telling what I have experienced of God, but to live the kind of life that you would expect to flow from it passes beyond risk into a kind of holy recklessness that is beyond me. If it is true about God, then, as my father said, there is nothing to worry about, not even death, not even life, not even losing the ones you love most in the world because, as Naya told me, no one is ever really lost. If it is true, you would live out your days as one who continues to be afraid of many things, but in the deepest, most final sense is without fear. That is a level of faith beyond my reach, but at least once in my life I caught a glimpse of it.

I was flying somewhere one day when all of a sudden the plane ran into such a patch of turbulence that it started to heave and buck like a wild horse. As an uneasy flyer under even the best of circumstances, I was terrified that my hour had come, and then suddenly I wasn't. Two things, I remember, passed through my mind. One of them was the line from Deuteronomy, "underneath are the everlasting arms," and for a few minutes I not only understood what it meant, but felt in my nethermost depths that without a shadow of a doubt it was true, that underneath, undergirding, transcending any disaster that could possibly happen, those arms would be there to save us if my worst fears were realized. And the other thing was a Buddhist metaphor that came back to me from somewhere. We are all of us like clay jars is the way I remembered it, and as time goes by, each jar gets cracked and broken and eventually crumbles away until there is not a single thing left of it except for the most important thing of all, the only thing about it that is ultimately so real that nothing on earth or heaven has the power even to touch it, let alone to destroy it, and that is the emptiness that the jar contained, which is one with the emptiness of all the other jars and with Emptiness itself. Nor is that Emptiness ever to be confused with nothingness, but is rather whatever of its many names we call it by—nirvana, satori, eternal life, the peace of God. Suddenly then, in that pitching plane some thirty thousand crazy feet up in the sky, I found myself not only not afraid of what was going on, but enormously enjoying it, half drunk on the knowledge that yes, it was true. There was nothing to worry about. There was no reason to fear. It was all of it, *all* of it, and forever and always, good.

■ ■ ■

The only sound I can hear is the ticking of the clock somebody gave me with Dorothy and the Good Witch of the North and Toto in the center and twelve others from the old movie to mark the circle of the hours. The books are all holding their tongues, and Jimmy's bronze head is speechless. Jamie and I stand on the beach together under a pale sky. My mother, granddaughter of Jules and Mattie, holds her flowers upside down in the lap of her white dress, and old Lear awakens from his madness to lay his hand on Cordelia's brow. The Buddha's hand is raised tall and slender beside my father's watch. Naya is for the moment nowhere to be seen, and not a creature is stirring, not even a mouse.

What is magic about the Magic Kingdom is that if you look at it through the right pair of eyes it points to a kingdom more magic still that comes down out of heaven prepared as a bride adorned for her husband. The one who sits upon its throne says, "Behold, I make all things new," and the streets of it are of gold like unto clear glass, and each of its gates is a single pearl.[11]

PART 3

REFLECTIONS ON SECRETS, GRACE, AND THE WAY GOD SPEAKS

A SECRET

There was no funeral to mark my father's death and put a period at the end of the sentence that had been his life, and as far as I can remember, once he had died, my mother, brother, and I rarely talked about him much ever again, either to each other or to anybody else. It made my mother too sad to talk about him, and since there was already more than enough sadness to go round, my brother and I avoided the subject with her as she avoided it for her own reasons also with us. Once in a while she would bring it up but only in very oblique ways. I remember her saying things like "You're going to have to be big boys now," and "Now things are going to be different for all of us," and to me, "You're the man of the family now," with that one little three-letter adverb freighted with more grief and anger and guilt and God knows what all else than it could possibly bear.

We didn't talk about my father with each other, and we didn't talk about him outside the family either partly at least because suicide was looked on as something a little shabby and shameful in those days. Nice people weren't supposed to get mixed up with it. My father had tried to keep it a secret himself by leaving his note to my mother in a place where only she would be likely to find it and by saying a number of times the last few weeks of his life that there was something wrong with the Chevy's exhaust system, which he was going to see if he could fix. He did this partly in hopes that his life insurance wouldn't be invalidated, which, of course, it was, and partly too, I guess, in hopes that his friends wouldn't find out how he had died, which of course they did. His suicide was a secret we nonetheless tried to keep as best we could, and after a while my father himself became such a secret. There were times when he almost seemed a secret we were trying to keep from each other. I suppose there were occasions when one of us said, "Remember the time he did this," or "Remember the time he said that," but if so, I've long since forgotten them. And because words are so much a part of what we keep the past alive by, if only words to ourselves, by not speaking of what we remembered about him we soon simply stopped remembering at all, or at least I did.

Within a couple of months of his death we moved away from New Jersey, where he had died, to the island of Bermuda of all places—another house, another country even—and from that point on I can't even remember remembering him. Within a year of his death I seem to have forgotten what he looked like except for certain photographs of him, to have forgotten what his voice sounded like and what it had been like to be with him. Because none of the three of us ever talked about how we had felt about him when he was alive or how we felt about him now that he wasn't, those feelings soon disappeared too and went underground along with the memories. As nearly as I can find out from people who knew him, he was a charming, good-looking, gentle man who was down on his luck and drank too much and had a great number of people who loved him and felt sorry for him. Among those people, however inadequately they may have showed it, I can only suppose were his wife and two sons; but in almost no time at all, it was as if, at least for me, he had never existed.

Don't talk, don't trust, don't feel is supposed to be the unwritten law of families that for one reason or another have gone out of whack, and certainly it was our law. We never talked about what had happened. We didn't trust the world with our secret, hardly even trusted each other with it.[12]

DEPRESSION

One of the most precious of the Psalms seems to be one of the least known as well as one of the shortest. It is Psalm 131. "O LORD, my heart is not lifted up," is the way it begins, "my eyes are not raised too high; I do not occupy myself with things too great and too marvelous for me."

To be in a state of depression is like that. It is to be unable to occupy yourself with anything much except your state of depression. Even the most marvelous thing is like music to the deaf. Even the greatest thing is like a shower of stars to the blind. You do not raise either your heart or your eyes to the heights, because to do so only reminds you that you are yourself in the depths. Even if, like the Psalmist, you are inclined to cry out "O LORD," it is a cry like Jonah's from the belly of a whale.

"But I have calmed and quieted my soul," he continues then, and you can't help thinking that, although maybe that's better than nothing, it's not much better. Depression is itself a kind of calm, as in becalmed, and a kind of quiet, as in a quiet despair.

Only then do you discover that he is speaking of something entirely different. He says it twice to make sure everybody understands. "Like a child quieted at its mother's breast," he says, and then again "like a child that is quieted is my soul." A kind of blessed languor that comes with being filled and somehow also fulfilled; the sense that no dark time that has ever been and no dark time that will ever be can touch this true and only time; shalom—something like that is the calm and quiet he has found. And the LORD in whom he has found it is the Lady Mother of us all. It is from her breast that he has drunk it to his soul's quieting.

123

Judas / Saul

REFLECTIONS

Finally, he tells us that hope is what his mouth is milky with, hope, which is to the hopelessness of depression what love is to the lovesick and lovelorn. "O Israel, hope in the LORD," he says, "from this time forth and for evermore." Hope like Israel. Hope for deliverance the way Israel hoped, and you are already half delivered. Hope beyond hope, and—like Israel in Egypt, in Babylon, in Dachau—you hope also beyond the bounds of your own captivity, which is what depression is.

Hope in the Father who is the Mother, the Lady who is the Lord. Do not raise your eyes too high, but lower them to that holy place within you where you are fed and quieted, to that innermost manger where you are yourself the Child.[13]

SUICIDE

The most famous suicide in the Old Testament is King Saul's. He was doing battle with the Philistines. The Philistines won the day. They killed his three sons, and he himself was wounded by archers. Fearing that he would be captured by the enemy and made a mockery of if he survived, he asked his armor-bearer to put him out of his misery. When the armor-bearer refused, he fell on his own sword (1 Samuel 31:4).

Judas Iscariot's is, of course, the most famous one in the New Testament. When Jesus was led off to Pilate and condemned to death, Judas took his thirty pieces of silver and tried to return them to the Jewish authorities on the grounds that Jesus was innocent and he had betrayed him. The authorities refused to take them. They said that was his problem, and Judas, throwing the silver to the ground, went off and hanged himself (Matthew 27:3–5).

Taking your own life is not mentioned as a sin in the Bible. There's no suggestion that it was considered either shameful or

124

cowardly. When, as in the case of Saul and Judas, pain, horror, and despair reach a certain point, suicide is perhaps less a voluntary act than a reflex action. If you're being burned alive with a loaded pistol in your hand, it's hard to see how anyone can seriously hold it against you for pulling the trigger.[14]

RAISED FROM DEATH

God knows we have our own demons to be cast out, our own uncleanness to be cleansed. Neurotic anxiety happens to be my own particular demon, a floating sense of doom that has ruined many of what could have been, should have been, the happiest days of my life, and more than a few times in my life I have been raised from such ruins, which is another way of saying that more than a few times in my life I have been raised from death—death of the spirit anyway, death of the heart—by the healing power that Jesus calls us both to heal with and to be healed by.[15]

TEARS

You never know what may cause tears. The sight of the Atlantic Ocean can do it, or a piece of music, or a face you've never seen before. A pair of somebody's old shoes can do it. Almost any movie made before the great sadness that came over the world after the Second World War, a horse cantering across a meadow, the high school basketball team running out onto the gym floor at the start of a game. You can never be sure. But of this you can be sure. Whenever you find tears in your eyes, especially unexpected tears, it is well to pay the closest attention.

They are not only telling you something about the secret of who you are, but more often than not God is speaking to you through them of the mystery of where you have come from and is summoning you to where, if your soul is to be saved, you should go to next.[16]

DYING

The airport is crowded, noisy, frenetic. There are yowling babies, people being paged, the usual ruckus. Outside, a mixture of snow and sleet is coming down. The runways show signs of icing. Flight delays and cancellations are called out over the PA system together with the repeated warning that in view of recent events, any luggage left unattended will be immediately impounded. There are more people than usual stepping outside to smoke. The air is blue with it. Once aboard, you peer through the windows for traces of ice on the wings and search the pancaked faces of the flight attendants for anything like the knot of anxiety you feel in your own stomach as they run through the customary emergency procedures. The great craft lumbers its way to the take-off position, the jets shrill. As it picks up speed, you count the seconds till you feel liftoff. More than so many, you've heard, means trouble. Once airborne, you can hardly see the wings at all through the gray turbulence scudding by. The steep climb is as rough as a Ford pickup. Gradually it starts to even out. The clouds thin a little. Here and there you see tatters of clear air among them. The pilot levels off slightly. Nobody is talking. The calm and quiet of it are almost palpable. Suddenly, in a rush of light, you break out of the weather. Beneath you the clouds are a furrowed pasture. Above, no sky in creation was ever bluer.

Possibly the last takeoff of all is something like that. When the time finally comes, you're scared stiff to be sure, but maybe by then you're just as glad to leave the whole show behind and get going. In a matter of moments, everything that seemed to matter stops mattering. The slow climb is all there is. The stillness. The clouds. Then the miracle of flight as from fathom upon fathom below you surface suddenly into open sky. The dazzling sun.[17]

MEMORY

There are two ways of remembering. One way is to make an excursion from the living present back into the dead past. The old sock remembers how things used to be when you and I were young, Maggie. The faraway look in his eyes is partly the beer and partly that he's really far away.

The other way is to summon the dead past back into the living present. The young widow remembers her husband, and he is there beside her.

When Jesus said, "Do this in remembrance of me" (1 Corinthians 11:24), he was not prescribing a periodic slug of nostalgia.[18]

REMEMBER

When you remember me, it means that you have carried something of who I am with you, that I have left some mark of who I am on who you are. It means that you can summon me back to your mind even though countless years and miles may stand between us. It means that if we meet again, you will know me. It means that even after I die, you can still see my face and hear my voice and speak to me in your heart.

For as long as you remember me, I am never entirely lost. When I'm feeling most ghostlike, it's your remembering me that helps remind me that I actually exist. When I'm feeling sad, it's my consolation. When I'm feeling happy, it's part of why I feel that way.

If you forget me, one of the ways I remember who I am will be gone. If you forget me, part of who I am will be gone.

"Jesus, remember me when you come into your kingdom," the good thief said from his cross (Luke 23:42). There are perhaps no more human words in all of Scripture, no prayer we can pray so well.[19]

FUNERAL

In Aramaic, *talitha cumi* means "Little girl, get up." It's the language Jesus and his friends probably used when they spoke to each other, so these may well be his actual words, among the very few that have come down to us verbatim. He spoke them at a child's funeral, the twelve-year-old daughter of a man named Jairus (Mark 5:35–43).

The occasion took place at the man's house. There was plenty of the kind of sorrow you expect when anybody that young dies. And that's one of the great uses of funerals surely, to be cited when people protest that they're barbaric holdovers from the past, that you should celebrate the life rather than mourn the death, and so on. Celebrate the life by all means, but face up to the death of that life. Weep all the tears you have in you to weep, because whatever may happen next, if anything does, this has happened. Something precious and irreplaceable has come to an end and something in you has come to an end with it. Funerals put a period after the sentence's last word. They close a door. They let you get on with your life.

The child was dead, but Jesus, when he got there, said she was only asleep. He said the same thing when his friend Lazarus died. Death is not any more permanent than sleep is permanent is what he meant, apparently. That isn't to say he took death lightly. When he heard about Lazarus, he wept, and it's hard to imagine him doing any differently here. But if death is the closing of one door, he seems to say, it is the opening of another one. *Talitha cumi.* He took the little girl's hand, and he told her to get up, and she did. The mother and father were there, Mark says. The neighbors, the friends. It is a scene to conjure with.

Old woman, get up. Young man. The one you don't know how you'll ever manage to live without. The one you don't know how you ever managed to live with. Little girl. "Get up," he says.

The other use of funerals is to remind us of those two words. When the last hymn has been sung, the benediction given, and the immediate family escorted out a side door, they may be the best we have to make it possible to *get up* ourselves.[20]

PEACE

Peace has come to mean the time when there aren't any wars or even when there aren't any major wars. Beggars can't be choosers; we'd most of us settle for that. But in Hebrew, peace, *shalom*, means fullness, means having everything you need to be wholly and happily yourself.

One of the titles by which Jesus is known is Prince of Peace, and he used the word himself in what seems at first glance to be two radically contradictory utterances. On one occasion he said to the disciples, "Do not think that I have come to bring peace on earth; I have not come to bring peace, but a sword" (Matthew 10:34). And later on, the last time they ate together, he said to them, "Peace I leave with you; my peace I give to you" (John 14:27).

The contradiction is resolved when you realize that, for Jesus, peace seems to have meant not the absence of struggle, but the presence of love.[21]

USES OF MEMORY

I am inclined to believe that God's chief purpose in giving us memory is to enable us to go back in time so that if we didn't play those roles right the first time round, we can still have another go at it now. We cannot undo our old mistakes or their consequences any more than we can erase old wounds that we have both suffered and inflicted, but through the power that memory gives us of thinking, feeling, imagining our way back through time, we can at long last finally finish with the past in the sense of removing its power to hurt us and other people and to stunt our growth as human beings.

The sad things that happened long ago will always remain part of who we are just as the glad and gracious things will too, but instead of being a burden of guilt, recrimination, and regret that make us constantly stumble as we go, even the saddest things can become, once we have made peace with them, a source of wisdom and strength for the journey that still lies ahead. It is through memory that we are able to reclaim much of our lives that we have long since written off by finding that in everything that has happened to us over the years God was offering us possibilities of new life and healing which, though we may have missed them at the time, we can still choose and be brought to life by and healed by all these years later.[22]

IF GOD SPEAKS

If God speaks anywhere, it is into our personal lives that he speaks. Someone we love dies, say. Some unforeseen act of kindness or cruelty touches the heart or makes the blood run cold. We fail a friend, or a friend fails us, and we are appalled at the capacity we all of us have for estranging the very people

in our lives we need the most. Or maybe nothing extraordinary happens at all—just one day following another, helter-skelter, in the manner of days. We sleep and dream. We wake. We work. We remember and forget. We have fun and are depressed. And into the thick of it, or out of the thick of it, at moments of even the most humdrum of our days, God speaks. But what do I mean by saying that God speaks?

He speaks not just through the sounds we hear, of course, but through events in all their complexity and variety, through the harmonies and disharmonies and counterpoints of all that happens. As to the meaning of what he says, there are times that we are apt to think we know. Adolf Hitler dies a suicide in his bunker with the Third Reich going up in flames all around him, and what God is saying about the wages of sin seems clear enough. Or Albert Schweitzer renounces fame as a theologian and musician for a medical mission in Africa, where he ends up even more famous still as one of the great near-saints of Protestantism; and again we are tempted to see God's meaning as clarity itself. But what is God saying through a good man's suicide? What about the danger of the proclaimed saint's becoming a kind of religious prima donna, as proud of his own humility as a peacock of its tail? What about sin itself as a means of grace? What about grace, when misappropriated and misunderstood, becoming an occasion for sin? To try to express in even the most insightful and theologically sophisticated terms the meaning of what God speaks through the events of our lives is as precarious a business as to try to express the meaning of the sound of rain on the roof or the spectacle of the setting sun. But I choose to believe that he speaks nonetheless, and the reason that his words are impossible to capture in human language is, of course, that they are ultimately always incarnate words. They are words fleshed out in the everyday-ness no less than in the crises of our own experience.[23]

LISTEN FOR HIM

The question is not whether the things that happen to you are chance things or God's things because, of course, they are both at once. There is no chance thing through which God cannot speak—even the walk from the house to the garage that you have walked ten thousand times before, even the moments when you cannot believe there is a God who speaks at all anywhere. He speaks, I believe, and the words he speaks are incarnate in the flesh and blood of our selves and of our own footsore and sacred journeys. We cannot live our lives constantly looking back, listening back, lest we be turned to pillars of longing and regret, but to live without listening at all is to live deaf to the full-ness of the music. Sometimes we avoid listening for fear of what we may hear, sometimes for fear that we may hear nothing at all but the empty rattle of our own feet on the pavement. But be not affeard, says Caliban, nor is he the only one to say it. "Be not afraid," says another, "for lo, I am with you always, even unto the end of the world." He says he is with us on our journeys. He says he has been with us since each of our journeys began. Listen for him. Listen to the sweet and bitter airs of your present and your past for the sound of him.[24]

A VISIT WE REMEMBER

It was thousands of years ago and thousands of miles away, but it is a visit that for all our madness and cynicism and indiffer-ence and despair we have never quite forgotten. The oxen in their stalls. The smell of hay. The shepherds standing around. That child and that place are somehow the closest of all close

God is. God comes.

encounters, the one we are closest to, the one that brings ᴜ closest to something that cannot be told in any other way. This story that faith tells in the fairytale language of faith is not just that God is, which God knows is a lot to swallow in itself much of the time, but that God *comes.* Comes here. "In great humility." There is nothing much humbler than being born: naked, totally helpless, not much bigger than a loaf of bread. But with righteousness and faithfulness as the girdle of his loins. And to us came. For us came. Is it true—not just the way fairytales are true but as the truest of all truths? Almighty God, are you true?

When you are standing up to your neck in darkness, how do you say yes to that question? You say yes, I suppose, the only way faith can ever say it if it is honest with itself. You say yes with your fingers crossed. You say it with your heart in your mouth. Maybe that way we can say yes. He visited us.

The world has never been quite the same since. It is still a very dark world, in some ways darker than ever before, but the darkness is different because he keeps getting born into it. The threat of holocaust. The threat of poisoning the earth and sea and air. The threat of our own deaths. The broken marriage. The child in pain. The lost chance. Anyone who has ever known him has known him perhaps better in the dark than anywhere else because it is in the dark where he seems to visit most often.[25]

THE TRUTH OF OUR STORIES

In the long run the stories all overlap and mingle like searchlights in the dark. The stories Jesus tells are part of the story Jesus is, and the other way round. And the story Jesus is is part of the story you and I are, because Jesus has become so much a part of the world's story that it is impossible to imagine how any of our stories would have turned out without him, even the

ho don't believe in him or even know who he
owing. And my story and your story are all
other too, if only because we have sung together
ayed together and seen each other's faces so that we are
at least a footnote at the bottom of each other's stories.

In other words all our stories are in the end one story, one vast story about being human, being together, being here. Does the story point beyond itself? Does it mean something? What is the truth of this interminable, sprawling story we all of us are? Or is it as absurd to ask about the truth of it as it is to ask about the truth of the wind howling through a crack under the door?

Either life is holy with meaning or life doesn't mean a damn thing. You pay your money and you take your choice. Only never take your choice too easily, of course. Never assume that because you have taken it one way today, you may not take it another way tomorrow.

One choice is this. It is to choose to believe that the truth of our story is contained in Jesus's story, which is a love story. Jesus's story is the truth about who we are and who the God is who Jesus says loves us. It is the truth about where we are going and how we are going to get there, if we get there at all, and what we are going to find if we finally do. Only for once let us not betray the richness and depth and mystery of that truth by trying to explain it.[26]

LET GO

They could hardly be a more ill-assorted lot. Some are educated, and some never finished grade school. Some are on welfare, and some of them have hit the jackpot. Some are straight, and some are gay. There are senior citizens among them and also twenty-year-olds. Some groups are composed of alcoholics and some, like the ones I found my way to, of people who have no alcoholic problem themselves but come from families who did. The one thing they have in common can be easily stated. It is just that they all believe that they cannot live fully human lives without each other and without what they call their Higher Power. They avoid using the word God because some of them do not believe in God. What they all do believe in, or are searching for, is a power higher than their own that will make them well. Some of them would simply say that it is the power of the group itself.

They are apt to begin their meetings with a prayer written by my old seminary professor Reinhold Niebuhr: "God, grant me the serenity to accept the things I cannot change, the courage to change the things I can, and wisdom to know the difference." They are apt to end with the Lord's Prayer: "*thy* will be done . . . give us *this* day our daily bread . . . forgive us as we forgive . . . deliver us." "To lend each other a hand when we're falling," Brendan said. "Perhaps that's the only work that matters in the end." As they live their lives, they try to follow a kind of spiritual rule, which consists basically not only of uncovering their own deep secrets but of making peace with the people they have hurt and been hurt by. Through prayer and meditation, through seeking help from each other and from helpful books, they try to draw near any way they can to God or to whatever they call what they have instead of God. They sometimes make serious slips. They sometimes make miraculous gains. They laugh a lot. Once in a while they cry. When the meeting is over, some of them embrace. Sometimes one of them will take special responsibility for another, agreeing to be available at any hour of day or night if the need should arise.

They also have slogans, which you can either dismiss as

Let Go

hopelessly simplistic or cling on to like driftwood in a stormy sea. One of them is "Let go and let God"—which is so easy to say and for people like me so far from easy to follow. Let go of the dark, which you wrap yourself in like a straitjacket, and let in the light. Stop trying to protect, to rescue, to judge, to manage the lives around you—your children's lives, the lives of your husband, your wife, your friends—because that is just what you are powerless to do. Remember that the lives of other people are not your business. They are their business. They are God's business because they all have God, whether they use the word God or not. Even your own life is not your business. It also is God's business. Leave it to God. It is an astonishing thought. It can become a life-transforming thought.[27]

LIFE-GIVING POWER

Most of the time we tend to think of life as a neutral kind of thing, I suppose. We are born into it one fine day, given life, and in itself life is neither good nor bad except as we make it so by the way that we live it. We may make a full life for ourselves or an empty life, but no matter what we make of it, the common view is that life itself, whatever life is, does not care one way or another any more than the ocean cares whether we swim in it or drown in it. In honesty, one has to admit that a great deal of the evidence supports such a view. But rightly or wrongly, the Christian faith flatly contradicts it. To say that God is spirit is to say that life does care, that the life-giving power that life itself comes from is not indifferent as to whether we sink or swim. It wants us to swim. It is to say that whether you call this life-giving power the Spirit of God or Reality or the Life Force or anything else, its most basic characteristic is that it wishes us well and is at work toward that end.

Heaven knows terrible things happen to people in this world. The good die young, and the wicked prosper, and in any one town, anywhere, there is grief enough to freeze the blood. But from deep within whatever the hidden spring is that life wells up from, there wells up into our lives, even at their darkest and maybe especially then, a power to heal, to breathe new life into us. And in this regard, I think, every man is a mystic because every man at one time or another experiences in the thick of his joy or his pain a power that comes out of the depths of his life to bless him. I do not believe that it matters greatly what name you call this power—the Spirit of God is only one of its names—but what I think does matter, vastly, is that we open ourselves to receive it; that we address it and let ourselves be addressed by it; that we move in the direction that it seeks to move us, the direction of fuller communion with itself and with one another. Indeed, I believe that for our sakes this Spirit beneath our spirits will make Christs of us before we are done, or, for our sakes, it will destroy us.[28]

THE FINAL SECRET

The final secret, I think, is this: that the words "You shall love the Lord your God" become in the end less a command than a promise. And the promise is that, yes, on the weary feet of faith and the fragile wings of hope, we will come to love him at last as from the first he has loved us—loved us even in the wilderness, especially in the wilderness, because he has been in the wilderness with us. He has been in the wilderness for us. He has been acquainted with our grief.

And, loving him, we will come at last to love each other too so that, in the end, the name taped on every door will be the name of the one we love.

"And these words which I command you this day shall be upon your heart, and you shall teach them diligently to your children, and you shall talk of them when you sit in your house, and when you walk by the way, and when you rise."

And rise we shall, out of the wilderness, every last one of us, even as out of the wilderness Christ rose before us. That is the promise, and the greatest of all promises.[29]

138

SOURCES

Beyond Words: Daily Readings in the ABC's of Faith. San Francisco: HarperCollins 2004.

The Clown in the Belfry: Writings on Faith and Fiction. San Francisco: HarperCollins 1992.

The Eyes of the Heart: A Memoir of the Lost and Found. San Francisco: HarperCollins 2000.

The Magnificent Defeat. New York: Harper & Row 1985.

A Room Called Remember: Uncollected Pieces. San Francisco: HarperCollins 1992.

The Sacred Journey: A Memoir of Early Days. San Francisco: HarperCollins 1982.

Secrets in the Dark: A Life in Sermons. San Francisco: HarperCollins 2007.

Telling Secrets: A Memoir. San Francisco: HarperCollins 1991.

NOTES

1. From *The Sacred Journey*, 37–58.
2. From *A Room Called Remember*, 1–12.
3. From *The Eyes of the Heart*, 1–7.
4. From *The Eyes of the Heart*, 8.
5. From *The Eyes of the Heart*, 11–24.
6. From *The Eyes of the Heart*, 60–62.
7. From *The Eyes of the Heart*, 76–81.
8. From *The Eyes of the Heart*, 146–50.
9. From *The Eyes of the Heart*, 153–62.
10. From *The Eyes of the Heart*, 165–68.
11. From *The Eyes of the Heart*, 170–83.
12. From *Telling Secrets*, 7–10.
13. From *Beyond Words*, 80–81.
14. From *Beyond Words*, 379–80.
15. From *Secrets in the Dark*, 151.
16. From *Beyond Words*, 383.
17. From *Beyond Words*, 87–88.
18. From *Beyond Words*, 252.
19. From *Beyond Words*, 342.
20. From *Beyond Words*, 122–23.
21. From *Beyond Words*, 307.
22. From *Telling Secrets*, 32–33.
23. From *The Sacred Journey*, 1–2, 3–4.
24. From *The Sacred Journey*, 77–78.
25. From *The Clown in the Belfry*, 124–25.
26. From *Secrets in the Dark*, 137.
27. From *Telling Secrets*, 90–92.
28. From *The Magnificent Defeat*, 114–15.
29. From *A Room Called Remember*, 45.

The Remarkable Ordinary

How to Stop, Look, and Listen to Life

Frederick Buechner

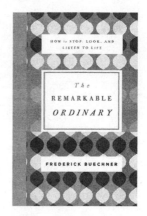

Your remarkable life is happening right here, right now.

You may not be able to see it—your life may seem predictable and your work insignificant until you look at your life as Frederick Buechner does.

Based on a series of mostly unpublished lectures, Frederick Buechner reveals how to stop, look, and listen to your life. He reflects on how both art and faith teach us how to pay attention to the remarkableness right in front of us, to watch for the greatness in the ordinary, and to use our imaginations to see the greatness in others and love them well.

As you learn to listen to your life and what God is doing in it, you will uncover the plot of your life's story and the sacred opportunity to connect with the Divine in each moment.

Pay attention, says Buechner. Listen to the call of a bird or the rush of the wind, to the people who flow in and out of your life. The ordinary points you to the extraordinary God who created and loves all of creation, including you. Pay attention to these things as if your life depends upon it. Because, of course, it does.

Available in stores and online!

ZONDERVAN®
.com